"In an era when highly edited versions of the self rocket through cyberspace via instant messaging, the meticulous empirical research of *Forging the Male Spirit* leads to a haunting but convincing counternarrative. Here young men yearn for slower, braver, face-to-face forms of intimacy with male peers and adult men. They find not in institutional religion but in ongoing same-sex support groups the true foundry of authentic masculine spirituality."

—Robert C. Dykstra
Princeton Theological Seminary
Coeditor of *Losers, Loners, and Rebels: The Spiritual Struggles of Boys*

"*Forging the Male Spirit* is an invaluable resource for anyone wishing to move from thinking to actually doing something about the spiritual development of college men. From broad surveys as well as detailed case studies of both persons and institutions . . . , we learn how we and our institutions can understand and . . . address men's concerns about their spiritualities and masculinities."

—Harry Brod
University of Northern Iowa
Coeditor of *Brother Keepers: New Perspectives on Jewish Masculinity*

Forging the Male Spirit

Forging the Male Spirit

The Spiritual Lives of American College Men

W. Merle Longwood
William C. Schipper, OSB
Philip Culbertson

To Jim —
Without your help
we'd have never have been
able to make this happen
at Siena. In friendship
Merle

WIPF & STOCK · Eugene, Oregon

FORGING THE MALE SPIRIT
The Spiritual Lives of American College Men

Wipf & Stock
An Imprint of Wipf and Stock Publishers
199 W. 8th Ave., Suite 3
Eugene, OR 97401

www.wipfandstock.com

ISBN 13: 978-1-55635-305-5

Contents

Contributors

W. Merle Longwood is professor emeritus of religious studies at Siena College in Loudonville, New York. He was founding co-chair of the Men's Studies in Religion Group of the American Academy of Religion and co-founded the men's spirituality groups program at Siena College. His previous publications include *Redeeming Men: Religion and Masculinities* and *Sexual Abuse in the Catholic Church: Trusting the Clergy?*

William C. Schipper, OSB, is director of Campus Ministry at Saint John's University in Collegeville, Minnesota. His doctoral thesis was entitled "Masculinity, Spirituality, and Sexuality: The Interpreted Lived Experience of the Traditional Age College Male." He has facilitated numerous groups of male students and has organized and directed over fifty retreats for college men. Fr. Bill teaches courses at Saint John's University focused on the sexuality and spirituality of the traditional age college male.

Philip Culbertson is an adjunct faculty member at both the College of the Desert in Palm Springs, California, and the University of Auckland in New Zealand. His previous publications include *New Adam: The Future of Male Spirituality*; *The Spirituality of Men*; *Caring for God's People*; *Spirit Possession, Theology, and Identity*; and *The Bible in/and Popular Culture*.

Gar Kellom serves as Director of Student Support Services at Winona State University in Winona, Minnesota, and has recently received a quarter-million dollar grant to fund Dads and Mothers groups for student parents. This work is an outgrowth of the research in this book and his previous publications, *Engaging College Men* and *Designing Effective Programs and Services for College Men*.

Preface

THIS BOOK AIMS TO assist colleges, universities, and others who are interested in encouraging increased authenticity and spiritual growth among traditional-age college men. We believe that young men change significantly during their college years and that best practices can be implemented that will facilitate the development of the spiritual dimension of their lives. As we discuss spirituality, which we will define more carefully in chapter 3, we are particularly concerned with the "big questions," which are essentially spiritual questions, that students wrestle with in this phase of their lives: Who am I and what do I believe? What are the deepest values that inform my life? What is my mission or purpose in life? What kind of person was I born to be and how can I become that person more fully? How can my inner life be nurtured and bonded with transcendent values and a vision of a larger whole? What sort of world do I live in and how do I want to help shape it into what I would like it to become? What kind of interconnectedness or wholeness is there between all things? Is this related to what some may call God, the life force, a higher power, ultimate reality, cosmic nature, or the Great Spirit? How do I move toward greater authenticity or to a more authentic self? What role does imagination play in bringing together insights, images, and ideas in my efforts at meaning making?

Our focus in this study is intended to answer the question whether traditional-age college men regard it as manly to be spiritual, or in other words, whether there is a connection between their masculinity and their spirituality. For the purposes of this book, we sought a broad definition of spirituality that would incorporate both the perspectives of persons anchored in various religious traditions and faith-based institutions that are accustomed to the language of spirituality, and of those who do not identify with established religions who would find words such as authenticity, purpose, meaning, integrity, wisdom, and values more comfortable as ways of expressing their commitments.

Chapter 1, "Recent Research on Emerging Men's Groups," was written by Gar Kellom, who directed a project involving fourteen colleges, and funded by the Lilly Endowment, that sought to explore how college men on those campuses understood vocation, spirituality, and gender identity. In developing the research to determine what was happening on those campuses, both inside and outside the classroom, Kellom used two empirical methodologies—James O'Neil's Gender Role Conflict Scale, and social norms research on masculinity and spirituality—to explore the interest that college men have in spirituality and also to assess the interest among college men in men's groups.

In chapter 2, "The Development of Men's Spirituality Groups on Campus: The Saint John's Experience," we have provided an extended case study of the Men's Spirituality Groups Program at Saint John's University in Collegeville, Minnesota, within an overall effort to reenvision the mission of that all-men's institution to be not just a college *of* men but a college *for* men. The model of spirituality groups that emerged at Saint John's has been adapted at a number of other college campuses. A variety of men's groups were formed on these campuses that encouraged men to tell their stories in confidential safe places, in which they developed enhanced self-understanding that was reflected in deeper and more satisfying relationships within the groups as well as with significant others outside the groups.

In chapter 3, "American Men, Religion, and Spirituality," we place the current discussion on spirituality within a broader context of how men have related masculinity, religion, and spirituality in previous times, especially in the twentieth century in the United States. In this chapter, we have also provided a working definition of "spirituality" to help us interpret the breadth of the experience of college men in relation to this dimension of their lives.

In chapter 4, "Masculinity, Spirituality, and the Measures of Being a Man," we provide a qualitative analysis of interviews with thirty-six college men on seven college campuses, who were recruited as part of this project. On the campuses involved—a subset of the fourteen campuses that were part of the Lilly Endowment project referred to in the first chapter—the men interviewed were asked to reflect on what "masculinity" and "spirituality" meant to them and the relationships between these concepts in their own experience.

Four of the colleges were affiliated with the Evangelical Lutheran Church in America—Augustana College in Illinois; Luther College in Iowa; Gustavus Adolphus College in Minnesota; and Wagner College in New York. Three were affiliated with Roman Catholic religious orders—Saint John's University (Order of Saint Benedict) in Minnesota; University of Portland (Congregation of the Holy Cross) in Oregon; and Siena College (Franciscan, Order of Friars Minor) in New York. We discerned some difference among the campuses in relation to how well the men interviewed understood the mission of their own institutions and its grounding in the values of the traditions underlying them, but that did not substantially affect how they responded to the questions we posed to them concerning their personal understanding of "masculinity," "spirituality," and the relationship between the two.

These seven colleges are small, private, liberal arts, four-year colleges with 2011–2012 overall costs in the range of $40,000 to $50,000 per annum (tuition, fees, room and board, books, transportation, and personal items). All thirty-six interviewees thus came from backgrounds of some financial privilege, or were high enough achievers to have been granted significant scholarships.

In our "Conclusion and Future Directions," we review some of the recent literature related to our study and summarize what we learned in this study, as well as identifying the implications it has for developing programs on campuses that can contribute to the holistic development of men, enabling them to be more integrated within themselves and in their relationship with others.

In the Appendix, we explain our research processes for those researchers who want to understand the methodology that informed the qualitative analysis that was used in chapter 4 to interpret the interviews we conducted on the seven campuses.

Finally, we have provided "Suggestions for Further Reading" for those whose appetites have been whetted in reading this book and want to explore more how spirituality relates to the experience of men, and of young men in particular.

1

Recent Research on Emerging Men's Groups

GAR KELLOM

THIS RESEARCH GREW OUT of a project funded by the Lilly Endowment to increase the number of college men involved in vocational discernment activities. Statistics on college volunteerism and participation in other experiential learning activities consistently show an imbalance, with 66 percent of the students participating in vocational discernment activities being college women and 33 percent being college males.[1] One purpose of this project was to improve that balance. Fourteen colleges and universities participated in the grant by creating pilot projects to experiment with different ways of increasing the percentage of young males exploring their identities through discussing the relationship between vocation, spirituality, and gender identity.

The fourteen colleges involved in the larger research project included Augustana College in Illinois, Davidson College in North Carolina, Duke University in North Carolina, Georgetown College in Kentucky, Gustavus Adolphus College in Minnesota, Hastings College in Nebraska, Hope College in Michigan, Luther College in Iowa, Morehouse College

---

1. Volunteering statistics from Campus Compact show that 35 percent of those volunteering are male, 35 percent of students studying abroad are male, and 36 percent of students enrolled in TRiO programs are male. TRiO programs are federal outreach and student services programs for students from disadvantaged backgrounds.

in Georgia, Saint John's University in Minnesota, Siena College in New York, the University of Portland in Oregon, Wabash College in Indiana, and Wagner College in New York. Our purpose was to identify the best practices for increasing male engagement in vocational discernment activities and to share the results at two conferences held at Saint John's University (SJU) in February 2008 and February 2009.

The first conference, in 2008, was for schools to share the pilot project ideas they were planning and to receive feedback from other schools on how best to accomplish their goals. The second conference, in 2009, was for schools to share the preliminary results of their projects and to look for similarities between schools in what we were finding. Several best practices were identified, such as targeting peer leaders who could influence increased involvement by male students, as were good ideas for how to recruit college men. We also wanted to design activities with and for college men in which they were more likely to engage. As we met, it became increasingly clear that involving key mentors in the projects was another form of best practice.

Some colleges, such as Hastings, Hope, and Morehouse, concentrated on ways to increase male involvement in the classroom. Others, such as Augustana and Luther, sought to increase male participation through Greek organizations or athletic teams. Our particular approach at Saint John's was to pioneer service and research trips to international locations such as Trinidad and Tobago, India, and Nepal, which in turn attracted additional funding from the ASIANetwork Freeman Foundation: Student–Faculty Research Program. These trips worked well over the past five years, with an all-male group of twenty participants in the first year and gender-balanced groups each year thereafter.

Georgetown College also offered adventure travel as well as microgrants for students to experiment with new ideas, and Davidson College offered funding for alumni/student road trips to bring generations together. Gustavus Adolphus College explored the mythological side of engaging college men in retreats with ritual activities and reflections from Larry Daloz on the meaning of male bonding and initiation. All schools shared their insights at the 2008 and 2009 Saint John's conferences during the process of development, leading to a very interesting dialogue among project leaders and participants.

What began to emerge at the first conference and continued in the second conference was a keen interest in the development of men's groups among all the participating schools. The University of Portland, Siena College, and Wagner College each tried a program of men's spirituality groups, using a model that had been successful for over ten years at Saint John's University. Morehouse College and Hastings College attempted pilot projects that were related to the curriculum or classroom settings, but these activities resulted in a significant movement toward the creation of men's groups. It wasn't long before we realized that we had another "best practice" emerging—the formation of men's groups—that would be noteworthy for conference participants to hear about and that needed to be more widely disseminated to higher education.

Academic Impressions, a visioning organization serving higher education professionals, picked up on the findings of the conferences and the project and asked that the best practices become the subject of web seminars in February and March 2009 and again in 2010. A lot of interest in these web seminars has been generated, with over 100 schools participating. A presentation at the National Association of Student Personnel Administrators (NASPA) in Chicago in 2010 attracted a packed house as well as the attention of the *Chronicle of Higher Education*. In 2011, Minnesota Campus Compact and Magna Online Seminars organized two more web seminars on the topic, Division IV-East of NASPA featured a presentation on this project at its annual conference, and another presentation was made at the annual conference of the American Men's Studies Association (AMSA).

The entire process was captured in a book published by the Men's Studies Press entitled *Engaging College Men*.[2] The concluding chapters of the book attempted to explain not only the complete set of best practices that had been identified but also what works and why. From those explorations of why some projects worked better than others, the research for this chapter emerged.

Basically, two research tracks were pursued to investigate the current state of college male behavior: administration of the James O'Neil Gender Role Conflict Scale, and social norms research on masculinity and on spirituality, including an assessment of interest about men's groups among college males. Both tracks produced interesting data that

---

2. Gar Kellom and Miles Groth, eds., *Engaging College Men: Discovering What Works and Why* (Harriman, TN: Men's Studies Press, 2010).

also helped to explain why college men would be attracted to men's groups and how to develop such groups to maximize their effectiveness.[3]

MASCULINITY RESEARCH

The first survey, administered to multiple entering classes, sophomore classes, graduating seniors, and some minority groups at Saint John's, as well as to students from a group of seven colleges participating in the Lilly Project, was developed by James O'Neil to measure the stresses of attempting to live up to traditional masculine gender roles. His Gender Role Conflict Scale (GRCS) has been administered to a broad base of men of all ages and backgrounds over more than a decade and provided a rich data pool to compare with our population of college men. Over 230 studies and twenty-five years of research have provided substantial support for the study of gender role conflict.[4] The wide use of the survey, as well as the many studies to support the validity of the findings, was attractive as we sought to use a well-respected tool to help us understand our small population of college-age men.

The GRCS is a survey of thirty-seven questions, divided into four subscales or psychological domains. The first domain, entitled Success, Power, and Competition/Control (SPC), describes personal attitudes about success pursued through power and competition. The second domain, entitled Restrictive Emotionality (RE), describes difficulties and fears about expressing one's feelings and the problem of finding words to express basic emotions. The third domain, entitled Restrictive Affectionate Behavior between Men (RABBM), describes limited ways to express basic emotions. The fourth domain, entitled Conflict between Work and Family Relations (CBWFR), describes difficulties in balancing work, school, and family relations, resulting in health problems, overwork, stress, and a lack of leisure and relaxation.

The overall results of the studies reviewed indicate that high scores on the GRCS are significantly correlated with numerous psychological

3. Steve Hoover, Chair, Counselor Education and Educational Psychology, and Tim Baker, Assistant Professor of Counselor Education, both of Saint Cloud State University in Minnesota, were invaluable in the development of the research tools and the data analysis for this project. Steve has presented the project at several conferences.

4. O'Neil has summarized this research in James O'Neil, Barbara Helms, Robert Gable, Lawrence David, and Lawrence Wrightsman, "Gender-Role Conflict Scale: College Men's Fear of Femininity," Sex Roles 14 (Nov. 5–6, 1986) 335–58.

problems for men. High scores are related to depression, low self-esteem, and stress. In the intrapersonal context, high scores on the GRCS have been associated with:

- Men's depression (RE subscale)

- Male college students' lack of well-being

- Shame and alexithymia

- Low ego identity and lower capacity for intimacy

- Problematic coping strategies

- Drive for muscularity and high-risk health behaviors

- Trait and state anger

- Helplessness, self-destructiveness, and suicide probability (RE subscale).

We are, then, looking at a serious matter. Further, in addition to the intrapersonal context, in an interpersonal context high scores on the GRCS have been related to:

- Dysfunctional patterns in interpersonal relationships

- Attachment problems

- Marital dissatisfaction

- Couples' dynamics and family interaction

- Sexual harassment, rape myth acceptance, and hostile attitudes toward women.

Taken together, the four domains on the GRCS describe traditional masculinity. Deborah David and Robert Brannon have also described traditional masculinity in terms of four stages that roughly align with those outlined by James O'Neil. Their first stage is "The Big Wheel," or always having to be in charge. Their second stage is "The Sturdy Oak," or never letting anyone see you cry. Their third stage is "No Sissy Stuff," which can be seen as closely related to O'Neil's scale concerning affectionate behavior between men. Their last stage is "Give 'Em Hell," or take it to the limit, or even put the pedal to the metal.[5] With the rough alignment of these two well-utilized versions of traditional masculinity, we felt comfortable that our research would help us identify where college men would rank themselves in terms of traditional masculinity.

SOCIAL NORMS MASCULINITY RESEARCH

Not only did we administer the survey to a wide-ranging group of college men to see where they scored themselves on the traditional scale of masculinity, we also asked them to score where they thought the typical college man would identify himself. This approach came from attending several social norms conferences and some consultation with Alan Berkowitz, a researcher and counseling psychologist, who urged us to research social norms masculinity.[6]

Social norms research started at Hobart and William Smith Colleges and focused in the early years on the perceptions and misperceptions that students had about the norms for drinking alcohol. A persistent and consistent misperception was discovered among college students about how much drinking was taking place on a campus. The number and amount that a student's peers were drinking was routinely overestimated, leading to increased drinking behavior by the student, reinforced by the belief that "everyone was drinking." Berkowitz charged us to see if there was a similar pattern with regard to masculinity and its resulting behaviors.

We devised the initial social norms masculinity survey by simply giving the survey twice to participants, instructing them to first answer the questions for themselves and then a second time for the typical male college student. We wanted to know to what extent Saint John's students resembled national samples of college men on the GRCS in the O'Neil database. We also wanted to know to what extent Saint John's University students displayed differences in the way they answered the survey for themselves or for the typical SJU student. We were optimistic

5. Deborah S. David and Robert Brannon, "The Male Sex Role: Our Culture's Blueprint of Manhood, and What It's Done For Us Lately," in *The Forty-Nine Percent Majority: The Male Sex Role,* ed. Deborah S. David and Robert Brannon (Reading, MA: Addison-Wesley, 1976) 1–45.

6. Alan D. Berkowitz visited Saint John's University as a consultant on several occasions for the Center for Men's Leadership and Service. He was invaluable in steering us in the direction of social norms masculinity research. He had been at Hobart and William Smith Colleges and helped to develop a social norms methodology.

that sharing the results of the survey with students in presentations or groups discussions could impact SJU students and their behavior related to what they perceived to be the social norms of masculinity on campus.

We began an ambitious longitudinal process by giving the survey to all male students entering SJU in the fall of 2004 and continued each year until the fall of 2008. We also sampled two of these classes in the sophomore year and one in the senior year to see if there was any change in the scoring over time. We also did several in-depth surveys, thanks to students in my Gender and Women's Studies course section on Men's Research, where the Caribbean international students and Latino men at Saint John's were sampled. One student from China translated the survey into Mandarin Chinese and administered it online to over six hundred college-age males in China.

Restrictive Emotionality

SJU Freshman, 2007; SJU Freshman, 2008; Caribbean Men, 2009

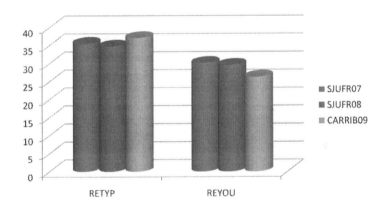

Of the thirty-seven statements on the GRCS, ten make up the Restricted Emotionality domain or subscale. Two sample statements from the subscale are: "Strong emotions are hard for me to understand" and "I have difficulty expressing my tender feelings." Students were asked to score their responses to all thirty-seven statements on the GRCS on a scale of 1 to 60, with agreement with the statement scoring the highest. They were instructed to respond to the statement for themselves and then the way they thought their peers would respond to it. Here is a sample of the results of the Restricted Emotionality domain from two freshman surveys and the Caribbean men. REYOU indicates the results of the respondent for himself and RETYP indicates the response the respondent made for the "typical student."

What we began to observe on every scale for every year that the survey was administered was a significant difference between the responses of the college men when they answered the survey for themselves and when they answered the survey for the typical male on campus. While there were slight variations in the strength of the responses each year, a consistent and statistically significant gap existed each year between the responses that students gave for themselves and those they gave for each other. This is often described as "I am willing to share my emotions but my friends sure are not."

At first, we thought this was a phenomenon among first-year students and that sampling sophomores or seniors would show a gradual amelioration in the gaps, but we didn't find that. Seniors scored themselves lower than their peers on the RE scale in 2009, but their score was almost identical to the first-year students and they still ranked their peers in the mid-30s on the scale, showing little or no change.

Restrictive Affectionate Behavior between Men

SJU Freshman, 2007; SJU Freshman, 2008; Caribbean Men, 2009

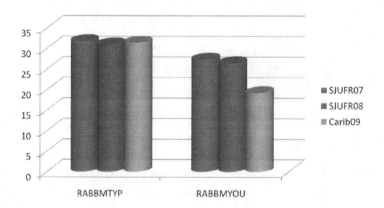

On the Restricted Affectionate Behavior between Men domain or subscale (RABBM), the pattern was the same. Eight of the thirty-seven statements make up this subscale and two of the statements were "Hugging other men is difficult for me," and "Affection with other men makes me tense." Again, students consistently ranked their agreement with these statements lower than they thought other men would answer. Here are some sample responses from two first-year classes and the Caribbean men:

Restrictive Emotionality

SJU Freshman, 2007; SJUFreshman2008:, Caribbean Men, 2009; 6 Colleges 2010

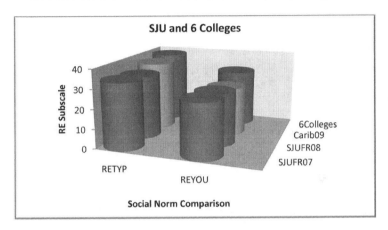

Upon discussion of these findings, what was fascinating was the process that the Caribbean men went through. As international students, they had the advantage of looking at their behavior and that of their peers in two cultural contexts. They recognized a significant difference between their behavior on campus and when they went home. In Trinidad or the Bahamas, they noted their extreme reluctance to express affection with other men, but when they returned to campus the same anxiety was not there, and there was a supportive environment to talk about it in class, in the men's center, or in the dorms. The misperception of the norm thus became obvious to them and, through discussions and being in men's groups with each other, they realized that sharing hugs and expressions of love and respect were welcomed and appreciated. Senior scores, by the way, were almost identical again to those cited above (30 for typical and 25 for self).

EXPANDING THE SURVEY TO MORE SCHOOLS

In 2010, we administered the survey, along with a social norms survey on spirituality, to a group of six colleges in the Lilly Endowment project to engage college men. By expanding the study to other campuses, we became convinced that the patterns observed on our campus were

Restrictive Affectionate Behavior between Men

SJU Freshman, 2007; SJUFreshman2008:, Caribbean Men, 2009; 6 Colleges 2010

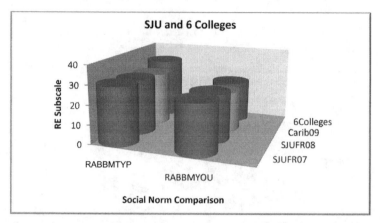

similar to those on other campuses as well. Here is a comparison of the results from above with the combined scores of the six colleges.

The schools included in this survey were Augustana College, Hope College, Luther College, the University of Portland, Wabash College, and Wagner College. While the overall scores of the schools on the RE scale are higher than those for Saint John's University, the gap between the scores given by the students to themselves are still lower (and by about the same amount) than the scores they gave to typical men on their campuses. This again indicates a misperceived norm. The pattern is similar on the RABBM scale (and the other two scales as well), with students scoring themselves lower across the board than their peers. An opportunity also arose to sample students and alumni from my college fraternity, Delta Tau Delta, which was struggling with how to organize its group formation activities. It is fascinating to me that the same pattern emerged from the fraternity brothers as we were seeing on our campus and other campuses. Here are some of the results.

INDIVIDUAL SCHOOL RESULTS

The six additional schools were able to obtain significant samples of the survey from male students, and while there were slight differences between schools, the pattern we saw at SJU still held. As there might be interest in looking at the data from the individual schools, included here are three looks at their data from three subscales of the GRC scale. This first example looks at the responses of students to gender role conflict

Success Power and Control

Six College Social Norm Comparison

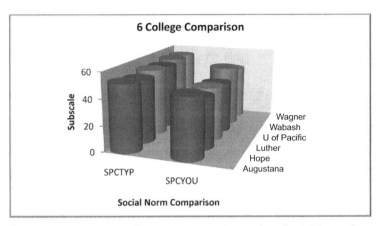

on the Success, Power, and Competition/Control scale. Male students at all schools consistently rated themselves lower on this scale than did the typical college male. Although the results were not identical, they were consistent in the lower ratings for self over other college men.

Another dramatic look at the data from individual schools is provided in the Restricted Emotionality Scale, which measures the conflict related to sharing one's emotions. It appears to be a good measure of adherence to traditional masculinity and shows even more dramatic differences between students' responses about themselves and how they think their peers would answer the questions.

Restrictive Emotionality

Six College Social Norms Comparison

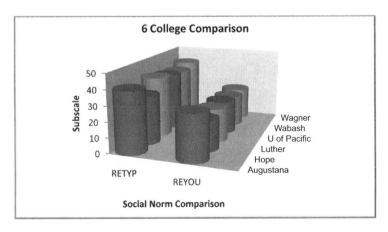

Restrictive Affectionate Behavior between Men

Six College Social Norms Comparison

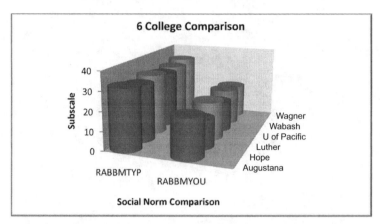

The last example looks at the most dramatic differences between the ratings of college men on their gender role conflict and that of typical college men on the Restricted Affectionate Behavior scale. There were significant responses from over 100 students at the first four schools and around thirty respondents at the last two, but the pattern still holds, so I have included them.

The few cases in which there was a slightly higher score for students about their own responses than what they perceived would be their friends' responses came from only two of the schools and pertained to only one of the scales: the Conflict between Work and Home Scale. I do not have great confidence that this scale applies meaningfully to college men, as they usually are not working full time and usually don't have families and homes. We could construct a measure of their conflict between studying and social life, but it would not be consistent with all the other O'Neil questions and scales. This scale is very important in measuring the gender role conflict of males in the work force and makes sense as one significant way to measure the impact of traditional masculinity on the lives of those men. I have not included the data here, as the results were not consistent and the meaning of the questions was ambiguous for this population.

SOCIAL NORMS SPIRITUALITY RESEARCH

Similar to the results with social norms, a spirituality survey seemed to provide data to support the best practices emerging from the Lilly

Endowment project and the topic of this book—that men's groups would be widely supported by college men on many campuses. We began piloting this survey several years ago with small groups on the campuses of Morehouse College, the University of the West Indies, and Saint John's University. We sought to discover whether there was a significant pattern of misperception with regard to spirituality similar to the one we were seeing with masculinity. The preliminary findings indicated that, indeed, there was a misperception, although it was the opposite of the masculinity perceptions. Where college men were ranking themselves as less committed to traditional masculinity than they thought their friends were, they ranked themselves as more interested in spirituality than they thought their friends were.

The Higher Education Research Institute had been doing an ambitious project, surveying the interest in religiosity and spirituality among college students, and was finding that, on average, over 70 percent of college students were interested in spirituality. This was higher than and distinct from religiosity or affiliation with organized religious institutions. The gender data showed that there was more interest among college women than among college men, but both ranked interest in spirituality as high.[7]

We decided to expand the pool of college men surveyed, to link it with the masculinity survey above, and to administer it to the same schools. We also added questions about interest in meeting and discussing the students' perception of and involvement in spirituality. The following graph summarizes those important questions: How important is spirituality to you and how interested would you say the typical college man is? How willing are you to share this interest and how interested is the typical college male? How willing are you to discuss this interest in some kind of group and how interested is the typical man? How interested are you in one-on-one interaction and how interested is the typical college man? Another group was added later to this study—my college fraternity—and we administered this survey to them to determine how interested they would be in groups organized around the theme of "brotherhood." "You at 6" refers to the self-report scores of those taking the survey at the six colleges, and "Typical 6" to the way in which the

---

7. Alexander W. Astin, Helen S. Astin, and Jennifer A. Lindholm, *Cultivating the Spirit: How College Can Enhance Students' Inner Lives* (San Francisco: Jossey-Bass, 2011).

Social Norms Spirituality

Four Questi on Survey of 6 Colleges and Delta TauDelta Fraternity

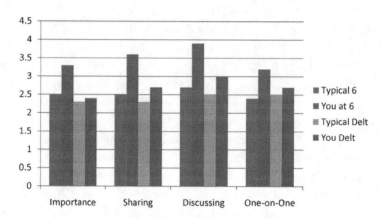

survey takers thought the typical student would respond. "You Delt" refers to the responses that college fraternity men in Delta Tau Delta gave for themselves and "Typical Delt" are the responses that Delta members gave for the typical man at their university.

As you can see, the pattern of misperception holds. On every question from every group, there was a significant misperception, and in each case, the young men answering the survey rated themselves significantly higher in interest than the typical college men they knew. The greatest scores for those being surveyed and the greatest differences between "You" and "Typical" were related to the question of sharing and discussing spirituality.

One might claim that this misperception of men's interest in sharing is limited to just talking about spirituality, but the case of the Delta Tau Delta fraternity indicates a broader interest in sharing and interaction. Not only was the survey administered to a group of active members in this fraternity, but I held a retreat with almost the entire chapter and a large group of alumni as part of an effort to chart the chapter's future. The retreat began with sharing the data from their surveys that showed the same patterns as the other men surveyed on the other campuses. The discussions were then enriched by personal stories from college men and alumni, who addressed the importance of the chapter to their lives. It was clear that this process opened the group up and redirected the course of the chapter.

Terry Franke, chair of the Board of Trustees of Lawrence University and an alumnus of Delta Tau Delta, summarized the results of the retreat this way: "Reenergized and repurposed—that is the best way to describe the Delts. They are now a group of guys who support each other, and where the fraternity house and the building were what they focused on, now it is the relationships not only with actives but with the alumni mentors." This demonstrates that the men's group is what is common to the experience. Rich Agness, chapter advisor, shared this experience and his perspective during the web seminar for Academic Impressions, and he is now working with key alumni to propose to the national fraternity officers that the process of initiation be altered to include some of the key elements of building successful men's groups. Perhaps this would be an improvement on or an addition to the important work of eliminating hazing from Greek initiation rituals.

The experiences accounted for above, as well as the masculinity and spirituality social norms research, both help to make a powerful case for pursuing men's groups in many different formats. The years of success with ongoing spirituality groups at Saint John's University, the new successes of spirituality groups at Wagner College, Siena College, and at the University of Portland, as well as the research previously done by Merle Longwood, Bill Schipper, and Mark Muesse, make a persuasive case for working to establish more such groups.

Add to this the dramatic results of fraternity men at Lawrence, and there is a compelling case for understanding not only what is going on with these groups but also how to work successfully to create them and sustain them on campuses.

In our work to present the early results of this research, we created a graphic to help isolate some of the key ingredients of successful groups and some ways in which these ingredients might interact. That graphic is below, and highlights four key elements: a confidential "safe space" for men to gather, skilled mentors or facilitators to help maintain that safe place, modeling how to share or open up and tell one's own story (i.e., disclose), and how to do active listening. When taken together, these elements create an atmosphere of trust in which deep friendships can thrive. What is *not* on this list is also interesting. We did not find readings or the discussion of articles or books to be particularly helpful. The text here is men's lives, a rich and never-ending source of material that all men seem to be able to relate to, no matter what generation. The

High-Impact Practices for MEN'S INVOLVEMENT

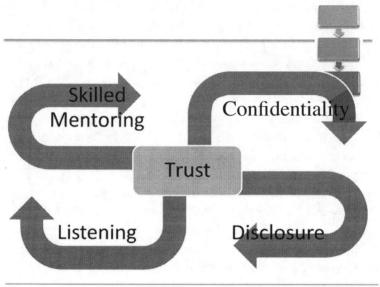

intergenerational sharing of our stories helps to bridge the age differences and highlights common themes of becoming men.

MORE EMERGING MEN'S GROUPS: MEN WORKING TO STOP GENDER-BASED VIOLENCE, AND DEVOTED ACADEMIC DADS

In addition to the men's groups that developed at the schools participating in the Lilly project on engaging college men in vocational discernment, two other significant groups of college men who were engaged in important work came to our attention. The first of these was the groups of college men who were working to stop gender-based violence. The second was the groups of students who are fathers, organizing to support each other in coping with the challenges of balancing parenthood and school.

Michael Kimmel, author of several books in men's studies and a frequent speaker on college campuses, approached me about a phenomenon he was noticing on many campuses he visited. He observed the spontaneous formation of men's groups working to stop gender-based violence and urged me to hold a conference for them at Saint John's to allow the groups to meet and work with each other and to gain support from some of the people working in our project.

In a matter of a few short months, we hosted a second conference at SJU in 2009 specifically to invite these groups, and over thirty such groups attended, comprising over two hundred attendees. The groups attending included A Men's Issue (AMI) from Syracuse University, New York; Male Athletes Against Violence (MAAV) from the University of Maine; Muslim Men Against Violence from Atlanta, Georgia; Minnesota Men's Action Network from Minneapolis; Fox Valley Voices of Men, from Wisconsin; A Call to Men: Ending Violence Against Women, a national network of college men; and Men Can Stop Rape, another national network. The gathering of these groups began to connect us to another fifteen groups, so we are now aware of at least forty-five such men's groups mobilized around violence prevention.

Those groups continued to meet following the Saint John's 2009 conference, met at a conference at Pacific Lutheran University in 2010, and attended the American Men's Studies Association conference in Kansas City in 2011. Ed Heisler, a graduate of SJU and staff person in a women's shelter in Duluth, Minnesota, developed the idea of studying this phenomenon and was able to complete fourteen interviews with male students at ten colleges and universities. A brief summary of what he found is included here as another way to make the case for the significance of men's groups emerging among college males.

Of the fourteen men interviewed, all but two strongly asserted that they would remain involved in gender equality and antiviolence work for the rest of their lives. For most of the interviewees, this work had become an important part of their identity and their life purpose. Some named it as a perceived calling. As these men described their efforts to stop gender-based violence, their paths suggested at least four common themes, listed below.

1. Knowledge about violence and an empathy for victims of violence motivated men to get involved. College men often described an experience in a class or workshop, or an experiential learning opportunity that helped to challenge their thinking and call them to action. For all but one of the men, their empathy was amplified by detailed knowledge of a woman they knew who had suffered male-perpetrated violence and gender inequality. Often, they were not aware of abuse that was impacting someone close to them until they were involved in these groups. The safe place offered by the associations frequently provided the opportunity to

make deeper connections between the work they were doing and the experiences of those close to them.

2. Groups provided peer support and the opportunity for the exploration of masculinity. Like the groups that emerged from the Lilly project, men working in groups to stop violence were often influenced by a strong leader, friend, close relative, or what we often called a "pied piper." Don McPherson, a gifted speaker and presenter on this topic from the world of Division I football and the NFL, was mentioned as a powerful influence. As with his presentations, the involvement of college men in these groups took them deeper into an understanding of masculinity.

3. Mentoring and intergenerational guidance and encouragement. Individual mentoring from adult leaders, as we discussed in our book *Engaging College Men*, also had a major impact. Many participants described an intense appreciation for the environment that allowed them to grow, the structure to develop their interests, and the resources to make a difference. Outside the groups, these men experienced a lack of support and some of the same difficulties and resistance that women often encounter in this work. Again, the group allowed participants a place to process their experiences of institutionalized sexism.

4. Self-improvement and altruism. Men involved in this work often spoke of the self-improvement it was affording them. A sense of altruism was a universal component of each participant's commitment. They shared a desire to make the world a better place. One of the men whom Ed interviewed said, "I'm making a difference and stepping outside the confined box of what it is to be a man and realizing that these are problems in our society that we need to tackle."

It appears, therefore, that like the men's groups formed to enhance vocational discernment in the Lilly project, men's groups formed to work for the purpose of stopping violence have some of the same key ingredients: peer leaders, skilled mentors, and safe places for men to process or work through their own issues and to build trust with those who have a similar interest in contributing to the common good. This phenomenon calls for additional study, but certainly indicates that men's groups are forming in many different contexts and that the college men who are participating are sensitive to the significant impacts of these groups on their lives.

THE MOST RECENT MEN'S GROUP:
DEVOTED ACADEMIC DADS (DADS)

In my new position at Winona State University (a state university of 8,000 students with a student body that is 60 percent women), one of the last things I expected to encounter was a men's group. As the Director of Student Support Services, I was hired to oversee a federal program focused on the needs of first-generation, low-income, and disabled college students. The history of the program indicated that for three decades, 75 percent of the participants had been women. The initial need that presented itself was the support of college men who were fathers. Based on the research we had been doing at Saint John's, I suggested that we form a fathers' group and, with very little encouragement from me other than providing some free lunches, the students quickly formed a men's group and named it DADs (Devoted Academic Dads). It has taken off.

Not only has the interest among male students continued to grow but student mothers have joined the group, reworking it into a Parent Support Services group with separate meetings for fathers and mothers and a combined meeting for all parents. One key issue is that students who are parents often feel that their fellow students do not understand or appreciate their situations and challenges, nor do many of their professors. They feel like "invisible students."[8] I included the DADs in the web seminars and presentations I did on the Lilly project, and men's groups formed to engage college men in vocational discernment or working to stop gender-based violence. National interest in this new form of men's group has emerged after every presentation. It seems we are bringing together a population of men that didn't usually meet before this.

Here are accounts by Bronson and Peter, two of the earliest founders of this group, as further proof that the phenomenon of men's groups is not only emerging in college student life but is also a good way to address issues that college men have in many areas. Bronson speaks first:

> While attending classes for my major of engineering, I would look around and see that my classmates were about ten years younger than me. They were worried about where they were go-

---

8. Research participant Bronson Mengedoht used that term to describe how college men he knows feel about being in school and being a parent. "No one really knows or cares what we are going through; they can't understand. It makes us feel as if what we are going through doesn't matter. This group has given me a place to talk about that and share my experiences with others who understand."

ing to drink that night. I, on the other hand, was trying to figure out how to pass my math class and what I was going to make my kids for supper. I needed more tutoring than I could receive at the Math Achievement Center, so I went to the SSS TRiO office. At one of the meetings, I sat beside Gar. He was interesting and easy to talk to. I made weekly appointments to talk with him, and those appointments usually ran longer than the time allotted. The student who had the meeting times after me was Peter. He had similar issues to mine, so we started combining our meetings.

From our early meetings discussing the troubles of being nontraditional students with children, we decided to form Dedicated Academic Dads (DADs). The group has grown considerably since our early days, but its mission—to provide a safe place for fathers to express their feelings and troubles while simultaneously giving us a way to become connected to the college community—has remained the same.

What is even more fascinating in the account from Peter Thompson below is how many of the dads in the group have come to understand gender role conflict and that what they are doing is redefining traditional masculinity and countering the misperceptions shown in the research above about what it is to be a man in our world today. They have not had the benefit of a men's center or a gender studies program to be introduced to the theory and research we have been discussing in this chapter, but their accounts are perfect examples of what we have found in other men's groups.

Peter said:

In the beginning, the creation of the Devoted Academic Dads, or simply "the DADs" as we've come to call ourselves, was almost accidental. Bronson Mengedoht had the advising slot with Gar immediately before mine most weeks, and when we realized that we were both discussing many of the same issues and concerns, we began meeting together. As a result of the similarities in the stressors we experience trying to reconcile our roles as student-parents with the commonly-held view of masculinity on our university's campus, forming this group was the next logical step. The primary purpose of the DADs group is to help us find the support and resources needed to simultaneously be better fathers and better students by creating a safe space where we can discuss the full emotional spectrum of our lives. By sharing things, ranging from the funny and uplifting stories about our children to supporting each other through the tough issues of child custody disputes and coparenting, we gain inspiration and knowledge from each other that helps lighten the burden many of us feel.

A lot of the stress felt as a father attending college stems from the disparity between our view of masculinity as fathers and how the general student body reflects the typical view of masculinity in our society. For us, our focus is on gaining a better education as part of our responsibility, not only to find careers that can support our families, but also to give our children a model of perseverance, dedication, and the ability to overcome the many obstacles encountered in life. In a sense, everything we do in life is as much for our children as it is for ourselves, which is a perspective many traditional students have a hard time relating to.

Both Bronson and Peter are articulate spokesmen for what the DADs groups do for them. They clearly appreciate the mentorship and the confidential safe space to air their concerns on parenthood as well as to work through the changing gender roles they are experiencing as men and as fathers. These two have also become pied pipers, attracting other college-student fathers who are wrestling with changing men's roles. Mothers have now been attracted to the group, which necessitated our forming a mothers' group as well as a combined group, yet the fathers still insist on their own gender-specific space to tell their stories and work on what it means to be a father these days.

CONCLUSION

Near the beginning of our work, during a conference at Morehouse College entitled "Where have the men gone?," Eddy Gaffney, the Dean of Students there, captured the essence of what I see us dealing with. He said, "You know what the problem is? Women's roles are changing. Therefore men's roles need to change." That was over a decade ago, and I have often thought of his words, since he passed away a few years ago, as each group of men meets to open up in a luncheon or afternoon conversation. It always seems that what is needed is just a safe space (or what someone has recently called a "brave space") where college men can say what is on their minds, no matter how ill-formed or politically incorrect, and get the honest and straightforward response of their peers and mentors on how to live their lives in a changing world.

The social norms research convinces me that we do not need to fear creating these men's groups or worry that some sort of animal-house behavior will result. Rather, I see men struggling with a way to be more honest with themselves—to speak from the heart about who they are and not what they think their friends want to hear. To me, the data are clear. While many men may live in a world described by Michael Kimmel as "Guyland,"[9] the concept is a college-age men's misperception perpetuated by the belief that other men endorse it when, in actuality, they don't. What is needed is a place to discover and give voice to the individual who is not the socially constructed man wearing a façade of traditional masculinity.

We have also shown that, contrary to the claim of Terrance Real, men *do* "want to talk about it."[10] They want and need to share their stories and process the changing social landscape. Men's groups, when done right—with the mentoring, confidentiality, trust building, and respect essential in all safe-space training—provide a passageway to adulthood. Nowhere is that more clear than in the fathers' groups. I asked Bronson and Peter one day about this developmental process and they said that what happened to them was almost instantaneous. One day they were guys involved in normal college male behavior and the next day they were fathers. "One day it is all about you and the next it is all about your child. You are no longer most important; she is."

Perhaps what has happened on college campuses and in society has been a dismantling of some of the places where younger men used to learn how to grow up and become a man. This is unfortunate, at the very time when such spaces seem to be needed to help them process the many positive and welcome changes that have empowered so many of their female classmates. If this chapter can help young men address the question of where they can go and who they can talk with in order to figure out how to respond to the changing gender roles of their time, then it will have served a useful purpose.

9. Michael Kimmel, *Guyland: The Perilous World Where Boys Become Men* (New York: HarperCollins, 2008). I have had conversations with Michael about the social norms view of *Guyland* and that what he is speaking and writing about is the mask of masculinity for boys and men in this stage. What is often overlooked is who these guys really are under their tendency to go along with the group

10. Terrance Real's *I Don't Want to Talk about It: Overcoming the Secret Legacy of Male Depression* (New York: Scribner, 1997) is another very popular book on men's studies that reinforces the idea that men don't want to talk about their interior lives. What this research shows is that men often *do* want to talk if they are provided with a safe and confidential space and with skilled mentors.

2

The Development of Men's Spirituality Groups on Campus

The Saint John's Experience

HAVING EXAMINED THE RECENT research on emerging men's groups, particularly focusing on the fourteen college campuses involved in the project "Increasing College Male Involvement in Vocational Discernment Activities," funded by the Lilly Endowment, we now turn to an examination of the pilot project that was developed at Saint John's University, as it was the first institution to develop men's spirituality groups. A careful review of the Saint John's experience will help us appreciate how developing spirituality and bringing a critical perspective to the dominant masculine ideals in American society was effectively accomplished by initiating a program that brought college men together in small groups to reflect on their lives. The groups enabled these men to challenge traditional masculine norms and to appreciate the importance of their own spirituality, helping them to realize their own potential in spiritual development and to go beyond beliefs that would regard paying attention to spirituality as inappropriate for "real men." We will show how this was done effectively at Saint John's University, as we turn now to describe how the men's spirituality groups were established there within the wider context of "The Saint John's Experience," which explored how college men, as men, were engaged academically as well as through programs designed to assist in their personal development.

ENGAGING MEN AS MEN: A BRIEF HISTORY OF DEVELOPING
GENDER CONSCIOUSNESS AT A UNIVERSITY FOR MEN

Saint John's University, located in Collegeville, Minnesota, is one of the
few remaining all-male institutions of higher learning in this country.
Established in 1857 by Benedictine monks from Germany, the university and its founding community, Saint John's Abbey, have a rich, inter-
twined history.[1] Today, about fifteen of the 150 monks from the adjacent
abbey live and work among the students of the university. The abbey's
bell banner is the tallest structure on campus and is the first thing one
sees upon entering the grounds of Saint John's. Although few students
attend the community prayers that punctuate each day, it is impossible
to ignore the ringing bells that call the monks to choir. The Benedictine
presence among the students of the university is almost inescapable.

In the 1960s, Saint John's University formed a coordinate relationship with the College of Saint Benedict, an all-women's institution,
founded in 1913 and located in the nearby town of Saint Joseph. Like
Saint John's, the College of Saint Benedict has a Benedictine monastic
heritage.[2] As a result of the coordinate relationship, the 1,800 men at
Saint John's and the 2,000 women at Saint Benedict's attend classes together on both campuses while maintaining residence in separate locations.[3] The significance of this joint effort was highlighted when the
institutions decided to hold an important retreat involving the governing
boards of both Saint John's University and the College of Saint Benedict
during the 1994–1995 academic year. Michael Kimmel and Elizabeth
Whitt were invited to serve as facilitators to help the boards explore the
implications of gender studies in the vision of these two institutions. The
boards reached a broad consensus that they would attempt to imple-
ment a gender studies perspective in three different settings: the all-male
residential campus of Saint John's University, the all-female residential
campus at the College of Saint Benedict, and in the coeducational classroom setting.[4]

1. "About CSB & SJU, Saint John's University." Online: http://www.csbsju.edu/
About/Saint-Johns-University.htm.

2. "About CSB & SJU, College of Saint Benedict." Online: http://www.csbsju.edu/
About/College-of-Saint-Benedict.htm.

3. "About CSR & SJU: A Unique Partnership." Online: http://www.csbsju.edu/
About.htm.

4. Gar Kellom, "The History of the Men's Project at St. John's University and the

Prior to this decision, the College of Saint Benedict had been providing leadership in educating women for decades, but Saint John's University had not articulated as clearly how it was providing a unique experience in educating men.[5] Given its two distinguishing characteristics—a Benedictine legacy and an all-male community—the time was ripe for the Saint John's community to begin reflecting more systematically on the relationship between them. This had begun in the 1980s, but it accelerated in the 1990s and continues to the present day. These are some of the highlights on that journey, listed approximately chronologically.[6]

From 1983 to 1987, initially with the assistance of a grant from the Fund for the Improvement of Postsecondary Education (FIPSE), Ozzie Mayers and Charles Thornbury, both professors of English, began to question how men's studies perspectives could become a meaningful part of the academic curriculum. In a variety of forums, they asked why the curriculum did not articulate men's issues as clearly as it had women's issues. This eventually resulted in the expansion of the Women's Studies minor to include a focus on men, leading to reconstituting the minor as Gender and Women's Studies, which later became a major;[7] the addition of a few courses on men's studies to the curriculum; and the creation of a Men's Studies Project with a national advisory board.

As part of the effort to build support for this expansion, Mayers and Thornbury developed a reading group for students, faculty, and staff that met for breakfast or dinner to discuss important works in the field of men's studies, such as *Contemporary Perspectives on Masculinity: Men, Women and Politics in Modern* Society by Kenneth Clatterbaugh; *American Manhood: Transformation in Masculinity from the Revolution to the Modern Era* by Anthony Rotundo; *Men's Lives,* edited by Michael Kimmel and Michael Messner; *The Rag and Bone Shop of the Heart* by Robert Bly, James Hillman, and Michael Meade; and *Men and the Water*

College of St. Benedict: The View from outside the Classroom" (unpublished paper, 1999).

5. Ibid.

6 Unless otherwise noted, the history of this development outlined in this and the following paragraphs is drawn from "Saint John's University Men's Center for Leadership and Service: Our History." Online: http://www.csbsju.edu/menscenter/history/history.htm (site discontinued).

7. "College of Saint Benedict & Saint John's University, Gender and Women's Studies." Online: http://www.csbsju.edu/gender-and-womens-studies.htm.

of Life by Michael Meade. This group dissolved after two years, as the energies of a number of its participants were redirected toward a variety of programmatic initiatives.[8]

Saint John's University and the College of Saint Benedict developed coordinate mission statements and now have a single academic provost,[9] but it is probably in the realm of the cocurriculum, developed especially through the Office of Student Development, that some of the most effective initiatives emerged concerning what it means for Saint John's to be one of only four all-male institutions of higher education in the country. When Gar Kellom came to Saint John's University as Vice President for Student Development in 1992, he worked with faculty, staff, and students to explore the meaning of its identity as an all-male institution with a Benedictine tradition dedicated to educating men in the latter part of the twentieth century.

In 1993–1994, Kellom joined Kathy Allen, Vice President for Student Development at the College of Saint Benedict, to begin a Portfolio Project to track the development of forty men and forty women over the course of their four years at the two institutions. The qualitative data they collected was analyzed by the social work faculty and summarized in a report, "CSB/SJU Student Portfolio Project: Senior Class Data and Analysis."[10] One of this report's conclusions was that at the end of their fourth year, 60 percent of the Saint John's students said they had "learned what it was to be a man at St. John's" and that a key influence in that learning for these young men had been the relationship they had developed with their monastic faculty resident.[11] This was regarded as particularly significant by the Monks' Men's Group, an advisory committee that had been formed to assist the Office of Student Development in its attempt to articulate more clearly how the Benedictine tradition can make a significant contribution in educating young men.[12]

In 1995, members of Saint John's Abbey developed an important paper, "The Relationship of St. John's Abbey and St. John's University: A Reflection," which sought to foster discussion as it described "how

8. Kellom, "The History."

9. "Provosts/Vice Presidents of Academic Affairs." Online: http://www.csbsju.edu/ SJUArchives/SJUHistory/SJUAdministrators/ProvostsandVPsofAcademicAffairs.htm.

10. This project was funded by a grant from the Kellogg Leadership Initiative.

11. Kellom, "The History."

12. Ibid.

values inherent in the monastic way of life apply to the wider arena of university life."[13] The Benedictine values lifted up were *lectio divina* (holy reading), monastic conversation (the way of life and the values set down in the Rule of Benedict), obedience (with its root meaning of "listening"), stability (of place and character), hospitality, and service. Reflecting on this paper, Kellom commented: "Missing from this document and from the mission statements of the university is any mention of men . . . Perhaps the most exciting part of the evolving project on men is the conversation with monks as we translate the wisdom of their tradition into the language of the men's movement or gender studies."[14]

An innovation that emerged from that conversation was the development of a lecture series focusing on "men's lives" in 1995–1996 that began with a theme of "Celebrating Men"—the theme chosen to emphasize positive aspects of men's experience rather than focusing on men as "the problem" or viewing men as the oppressors of women. The theme was changed the second year to "Telling Men's Stories," the name change being influenced by storyteller Michael Meade as well as by a group of monks at Saint John's Abbey who had illustrated in the last offering during the first year's series that an autobiographical approach can be an effective way to explore men's experience. Subsequently, the series became known simply as "The Men's Lives Series," taking its name from Kimmel and Messner's book, *Men's Lives*.[15] In its first year, the series sponsored nine events and, as it continued, it brought scholars to the campuses from various fields from around the nation, seeking through diverse offerings to provide men with "the opportunity to integrate spiritual, psychological, physical, emotional, and intellectual selves and to use this self-understanding as a basis for taking action in the world."[16]

Frequently, campus initiatives were developed in conjunction with the themes in the series from year to year. For example, in 1999, Tony Lanzillo, founding director of the Center for Men's Health Center in Camden, New Jersey, gave a lecture on "Breaking Down: Men's Health &

13. "The Relationship of St. John's Abbey and St. John's University: A Reflection" (unpublished paper, 1995).

14. Kellom, "The History." See further reflections on this issue by Aaron Raverty, "Are We Monks, or Are We Men? The Monastic Masculine Gender Model according to the Rule of Benedict," *Journal of Men's Studies* 14, no. 3 (Fall, 2006) 269–91.

15. Kellom, "The History."

16. "Men's Center of Leadership and Service, Men's Lives Series." Online: http://www.csbsju.edu/menscenter/mls/default.htm (site discontinued).

the Masculine Mentality," and subsequently, Michael Kimmel spoke on "Men's Bodies and Masculinity." These lectures caught the attention of Michael Ewing in Saint John's Counseling Center, and he and others began to give increased attention to men's health issues. This evolved into a longer-term research project that collected data on men's health at Saint John's University, with the goal of finding ways to use the data to change the behavior of men by educating them toward healthier lifestyles.

Considerable interest developed in the extensive work of the men's health educator, Will Courtenay, who was a speaker in the Men's Lives lecture series during the 2000–2001 academic year, thus further stimulating the development of a men's health initiative. This involved many students and spawned a proposal for hosting a national men's health conference as well as a proposal by the Physical Education department for a new lifestyle fitness class for both men and women, opening the possibility of addressing men's health issues through a required course in the academic curriculum. The university hired a health educator, Lori Kalpperich, to direct the men's health research project, to write grants, and to develop other efforts to educate men about health issues. To expand on this theme, in the spring semester of 2001, the Men's Lives series invited Sam Femiano, a clinical psychologist in private practice in Northampton, Massachusetts, to talk to the monastic community as well as the student body about his previous experience in a monastic community and what it meant for the work he subsequently developed with nonmonastic men. With a grant from the Bush Foundation that Saint John's University and the College of Saint Benedict received to create learning communities, Saint John's created a health and wellness floor, which expanded to a project in which first-, second-, third-, and fourth-year groups of students were formed to encourage participants who were living together to pursue healthy lifestyles.[17]

Early on, Janet Hope, of the Sociology Department, did an analysis of the lecture series and its impact on student learning in addition to conducting a survey of interest in men's studies among students. She presented her findings within the Men's Lives series, "Men's Issues—Where We've Been, Where We're Going," in the spring of 1997. She identified areas of interest for inviting speakers, which helped to guide the continuation of the series, and she noted that there was significant interest in men's studies within the student body among both men and women,

17. Kellom, "The History."

but she cautioned that not enough members of the faculty seemed willing to teach such courses.[18] Others raised questions about how well the presentations by the outside speakers in the series had been integrated into courses on the campus.

In the fall of 1995, Kellom gathered together a group of eight monks from the abbey to consider the question, "What contribution can a Benedictine community of men make in the area of men's development?" This small group, most of whom lived and worked among the students of the university, met regularly to discuss this question. These discussions led the group to conclude that the greatest contribution the community of monks could make would be to enhance male spiritual development. However, in order to assist other men, the members of the group realized they would need to understand more deeply their own spiritualities. They thus decided to spend another year sharing their spiritual autobiographies with one another. During this year, each member told the story of his spiritual development, highlighting the people and events that had most significantly shaped him.[19]

As an expansion of the lecture series, Charles Thornbury invited the National Organization for Men against Sexism (NOMAS) to hold its 22nd Men and Masculinity Conference on the campus of Saint John's University, in July 1997. He served as the chairperson of the conference that focused on the theme "Spirituality, Community, & Social Change." A number of faculty and staff from Saint John's University and the College of Saint Benedict participated in the program at this conference, including several of the monks of the Saint John's Abbey,[20] who expanded on the presentation they had made as the concluding event in the first year of the Men's Lives series on campus, "Personal Stories of Monastic Religious Experience: Is There a Men's Spirituality?"[21]

This experience of sharing their stories with each other had such a powerful effect on the men who had gathered over the previous two years that they decided it would be worthwhile to form groups for

---

18. Ibid.

19. Ibid.

20. Brochure, "22nd Men and Masculinity Conference: Spirituality, Community, & Social Change," Saint John's University, Collegeville, Minnesota, July 1997, sponsored by the National Organization for Men against Sexism.

21. "Men's Center for Service and Leadership, Men's Lives Series." Online: http://www.csbsju.edu/menscenter/mls/default.htm (site discontinued).

students at Saint John's, using their group experience as a prototype. In the fall of 1997, two student spirituality groups were begun under the auspices of the Office of Student Development. Each group was comprised of six to eight first-year men and two facilitators who had been members of the original group of monks. Although the creators of the student spirituality groups were initially unsure how this experiment would turn out, it soon became apparent that students had a positive experience comparable to what the monks themselves had previously. The response of the students within these groups was so positive that soon new groups were established. By the fall of 2011, the program had grown to about sixteen active groups, with three to four new groups of first-year students organized each fall semester. An evaluation of their impact will be presented in a later section of this chapter. This program has attracted national attention, and in 2003 it was recognized by the American College Personnel Association with its Outstanding Men's Program Award.

An important means of articulating the integration of Benedictine values into the education of the students at Saint John's University occurred through the implementation of a brief paper, originally drafted by Thornbury, and revised by a group of faculty, staff, and students into a one-page document, "Educating Young Men: Gender Education at Saint John's University; A Working Document" in 1998.[22] This statement sought to articulate Saint John's commitment to educating young men in the context of its coordinate relationship with the College of Saint Benedict, emphasizing how Benedictine values influence Saint John's commitment to educating young men, and what Saint John's expects young men to learn about themselves as men during their college careers. The student senate of Saint John's worked to rewrite this statement from a values perspective, and in this process it began to assume ownership of this way of understanding the self-development of young men.[23]

Another assessment of the role that Benedictine values play in the life of Saint John's University students was provided by Heidi Harlander, who studied the development of leadership among the students at Saint John's University. She described the Benedictine monastics as a "donor society," who "represent implicit cultural values, and beliefs,

22 "Educating Young Men: Gender Education at Saint John's University: A Working Document" (unpublished draft paper, August 7, 1998).

23. Kellom, "The History."

thus making them tangible to the students." They are "visible reminders and teachers of institutional culture, including socially responsible leadership." Specifically, she observed that the students' faculty residents were a powerful influence in their learning "the values of community, listening, respect for and sensitivity to others, responsibility, individual and community accountability, service, and stewardship." She noted that in commenting about the faculty residents, one student had remarked: "The leadership from the monks are [sic] very person-centered; they don't focus on a type of skill, like in government or that sort of thing, it's not based on climbing any sort of ladder, it's more like developing your skills as a person. That includes your spirituality and actually being the person that you can [be], actually living out the ideal that you say you have."[24]

A student initiative called the Saint John's Experience Project, also supported by the Office of Student Development, began in 2000. In this project, an evolving group of students conducted a variety of surveys on campus to attempt to articulate how students understand their experience as men who have been attending Saint John's University. Acknowledging that Saint John's is a rural, all-male, Benedictine and Catholic liberal arts college, the students in this project attempted to articulate what is special and unique about the experience that this institution offers to young men.[25] Students participating in the Saint John's Experience Project have shared their insights in a variety of forums, including making presentations at American Men's Studies Association conferences and in the university's own Men's Lives series.[26]

In 2001, the Saint John's University Center for Men's Leadership and Service was established, the first of its kind on an undergraduate college campus. Its mission statement declared: "Through research, education, and understanding, we strive to . . . create a more enlightened concept

24. Heidi Sue Harlander, "Men and Leadership" (excerpts from "Institutional Culture and the Development of Socially Responsible Leadership among Male College Undergraduates," an unpublished Master's thesis submitted to the Graduate School of the University of Minnesota, June, 1998).

25. "Men's Center for Service and Leadership, Saint John's Experience." Online: http://www.csbsju.edu/menscenter/projects/sjexperience.htm (site discontinued).

26. One example is a paper, "The St. John's Difference: Students' Perspectives of a Post-Secondary Environment Designed for Men," presented by two seniors, Bryan M. Bohlman and Matthew S. Steele, at the American Men's Studies Association annual conference in Albuquerque, New Mexico, on March 24, 2001 (unpublished paper).

of manhood informed by our Benedictine values. Acknowledg[ing] our roots with those before us who struggled for the liberation of all people, we seek to work for justice and to better the lives of men and women through innovative programs, scholarship, and service."[27] Among the projects it has sponsored—some of which had previously existed and were brought under the umbrella of the men's center—are the African American Men's Project; the International Men's Stories Project; studies on Caribbean men, 600 Chinese men, and Latino men; the AMES Saturday School Project (involving grade school students in Saint Paul); seven Annual Conferences on the College Male, the last of which invited men's groups that work to stop gender-based violence; Benedictine Leadership and Values Clarification; Collaboration with the Women's Center at the College of Saint Benedict, the Gender and Women's Studies Program, the Eugene J. McCarthy Center for Public Policy and Civic Engagement, and the Centre for Gender Studies at the University of the West Indies; the Father's Project; two coed service trips to Trinidad and Tobago to work with HIV-infected orphans; an all-male service trip to India and Nepal; a student research trip to Nepal, funded by the ASIANetwork Freemen Student Faculty Fellowship program; two coeducational service and research trips to India and Nepal to study the vocational discernment of Tibetan monks; Jim Smith's Athletic Leadership and Service; research and publication projects, which included an edition of the *Journal of Men's Studies* profiling the Men's Center research, and a New Directions for Student Services series book, published by Jossey-Bass; the Men's Lives series; Morehouse College Exchange Program; and the Saint John's Experience Project.[28] Harry Brod, a well-known men's studies scholar, was Scholar in Residence, sponsored by the Men's Center in spring semester, 2005. In 2007, the Men's Center obtained a grant from the Lilly Endowment to initiate pilot projects on fourteen campuses, focusing on "Increasing College Male Involvement in Vocational Discernment Activities."

Other developments included the creation of the Outdoor Leadership Center, acknowledging that men enjoy doing things outdoors;

27. "Men's Center for Leadership and Service, Our Mission." Online: http://www.csbsju.edu/menscenter/ (site discontinued).

28. "Men's Center for Leadership and Service, Projects." Online: httpp://www.csbsju.edu/menscenter/projects/Projects.htm (site discontinued). Also, e-mail correspondence from Gar E. Kellom, August 9, 2010.

increasing student senate involvement in the Men's Health and Men's Lives projects; two papers, "Improving the Recruitment, Education and Retention of Men in Residential Colleges and Universities" and "Serving Men Effectively in Residential Colleges," presented by Gar Kellom at the Oxford International Roundtable; and participation in a first-ever meeting of men's colleges at Morehouse Research Institute in Atlanta, with a special focus on concern for the decreasing percentage of men graduating from colleges and universities in this country. With encouragement from the Parent Committee, a father/son event was initiated to complement the mother/son dance and father/daughter events already in existence.[29]

THE FORMATION OF MEN'S SPIRITUALITY GROUPS

In the fifteen years since the men's spirituality program began, a variety of ways of recruiting men to participate in these groups has been tried. At times, all entering students at Saint John's were invited to join a spirituality group. Over the summer prior to matriculation, first-year men received a brochure describing the spirituality group program at the university. In the fall, a campus-wide notice was posted, and e-mails describing the groups and inviting participation were sent to all first-year students.

A more effective means of recruitment, especially in drawing in men who were not conventionally "religious," has been to use a process of recommending students as potential participants in the groups. One way this has been done has been to ask the faculty resident monks who live on each freshman floor, about mid-October, to recommend students whom they believed might be interested in and who might benefit from being involved in such groups. Alternatively, and sometimes concurrently, first-year symposium instructors were asked to recommend students they believed would be good participants. In addition to these formal structures aimed at identifying potential participants, a less formal and highly effective means of recruitment has been by word of mouth. Because current members of groups often speak favorably of their group experience in casual conversations with other students, word of mouth has been an important means of recruitment.

---

29. "Men's Center for Leadership and Service, Our History." Online: http:/www .csbsju.edu/menscenter/history/history.htm (site discontinued).

Facilitators have been recruited in a variety of ways, usually because they have been identified by the coordinator of the project or current group facilitators as persons who would likely be effective in working with students within these structured groups. Almost all the group facilitators have served in pairs, and initially almost all the facilitators were monks. Currently, however, five nonmonastic staff and faculty have been invited to serve as facilitators, usually along with a monk. The criteria used to recruit facilitators have been to find men who feel comfortable sharing their personal stories and faith journeys, who have an interest in and are likely to be effective in working with college men, and who also are skilled in respectful listening and teasing out issues that surface during group conversations.

Once groups were formed, the facilitators were responsible for the coordination of meeting times and establishing the initial group dynamic. Facilitators acted as role models within their groups, encouraging group members to pay attention to group dynamics and to speak in the first person, to give priority to attending the group meetings, and to share information from their own lives in a manner that assumed that what was presented would be maintained confidentially within the confines of the group. In the groups that have had the greatest success in moving deeply into life-sharing, the facilitators have been full participants, reflecting openly about their own struggles and relationships, all the while assisting others to explore theirs in the dynamics that occur within the groups.

Regardless of what means have been used for participant recruitment, the men's spirituality program often held an informational dinner for all prospective and active group members in early November. The dinner provided opportunities for prospective members to talk informally with active group members, to meet some of the facilitators, to ask questions, and to gather information so they had a solid basis for deciding whether they wanted to commit to joining a group. Students who were active in a group shared first-hand information about their experience with new students. The sharing of personal experiences by current group members has been the most effective means for recruiting new group members. Because participation in the spirituality groups demands a long-term commitment (four years) and requires a willingness to risk self-revelation, prospective students needed to gain as much understanding of the program as possible in order to make informed decisions about their own participation.

The program's administrators have recognized that spirituality groups may not suit everyone and that some students' spiritual needs might be better served through other programs at the university, such as Bible studies or retreats sponsored by the campus ministry. Occasionally, groups have been formed for students in their sophomore year if a sufficient number of students asked for this to happen, and some groups who have lost students via attrition sometimes recruited additional students at their grade level to keep their groups viable.

Group Meetings

Although they set their own schedules, new groups normally met for the first time just before Thanksgiving break. Those who volunteered to be part of a group were assigned to a specific group, and the size of each group was limited to ten students and two facilitators. This size was especially important for the groups that focused on one of its members' stories at each meeting, so that in the course of the academic year each group member would have had a full meeting devoted to his "story." This group size also allowed for the possibility of some attrition from students who decided not to continue their involvement or who left the university before they had completed four years there. It was also important to have a large enough group that it would withstand the temporary shrinkage likely to happen during students' junior year, the year in which some group members opted to study abroad.

At the first meeting, facilitators emphasized the importance of confidentiality, commitment, and communication, attempting to create an atmosphere that religious studies scholars might call "sacred time and sacred space." From time to time, the importance of these guiding principles was rearticulated within the groups. Confidentiality is essential to building trust in the group and it was stressed from the outset. Each member agreed that all personal information would be kept strictly within the group, so that nothing of the specifics of group activities would be shared with persons outside the group without the permission of the concerned group member(s). This made it possible for group members to feel safe in sharing some of the most difficult parts of their personal histories within the group. Members were asked to communicate honestly and openly, even as they expanded their comfort zones. In all of their comments, they were encouraged to speak in the first person, taking personal ownership of feelings, fears, learning, and experiences. Drawing on the Benedictine value of "stability," if not always naming it as such, group members were asked to commit to stay with the same group throughout their college years and to give priority to attendance at group meetings. If a member was unable to attend, he was to notify one of the facilitators or another group member to explain the reason for his absence. Being together for four years in a group allowed individuals within the group to interact, grow, and deepen in their relationships. As their bonds of safety and trust provided the parameters of their experience together, in the most effective of the groups, group members realized that they were able to participate in ever-deepening levels of sharing within a type of covenant that opened members to ways to resolve conflicts within the group and to grow individually and together toward maturity.

In the earliest years of the program, most of the groups met once a month, but increasingly the group members expressed a desire to meet more often. Now, typically, most of the groups meet every two or three weeks for about an hour, but some groups meet weekly. Some groups dine together; some groups include pizza and soda in their group meetings; some groups organize cookouts from time to time; other groups do not have any shared food or drinks associated with their meetings. Although the groups have had different formats for their meetings, some dealing with topics as they are raised by the group members from meeting to meeting, more often each group meeting has focused on one of its members who has told his personal story in response to a broad question that has been agreed upon by the group in order to initiate the discussion. When he has finished telling his story, other members often asked questions for clarification. Then they commented on the parts of that particular individual's story that most affected them. One might have said, for example, "I could identify with what you said about the difficulties you have had in trying to get closer to your father. I am also struggling to try to understand and get to know my dad now that I am at this new stage in my life."

Two powerful dynamics emerged from this format of sharing stories and opening oneself to questions and comments afterwards. First, this way of communicating enabled young men to open themselves to discuss serious personal issues in their own lives, moving beyond the topics of sports, politics, and sex—the usual range of topics that get discussed when men talk with other men. The groups were especially attractive for men with no formal religious background or men who were undergoing a critical examination of the religion of their upbringing. In fact, at one particular session arranged to evaluate what was happening in the men's spirituality program, long-term facilitators asked whether there had been a shift in the type of students who had chosen to join the spirituality groups, noting that the recently recruited students tended to be more stereotypically "religious" and therefore less interesting group participants. These facilitators noted that students' autobiographical stories and questions posed to each other in the groups were less dramatic and probing and more focused on factual issues and "safe" topics. In response, the administrator of the program at that time indicated that fewer students than usual had come into the program through nominations by faculty residents and freshman symposium leaders and more had come as a result of a follow-up general invitation that he had initiated.

One student commented that the spirituality groups "take the pressure off feeling you have to have it all figured out." Group members have routinely commented that they looked forward to presenting to the group because it was a unique experience to have several other men, mostly peers, really listen to what they had to say on matters of significant personal importance. Feeling that one is being heard in a nonjudgmental and confidential forum contributed decisively to developing a positive and open atmosphere in the groups.

The second powerful dynamic has been that group members reflected on how another man's story had triggered similar or different reactions within themselves. If the experience was similar, it was affirming to know that other men had similar experiences. If the reaction was different, horizons were expanded to reveal new or different possibilities for processing one's inner life, opening up the opportunity for new understandings of self and others. This forum allowed young men to acknowledge that they often had the same fears, joys, and challenges as their peers; sharing these aspects of themselves with other men was usually a broadening experience. This process allowed men to raise questions within themselves that they had not previously pondered or had not yet been able to articulate fully.

Group Development over the Collegiate Career

As indicated earlier, the groups did not all follow the same format, but the large majority of the groups had a format similar to the one that will be described here. During each of the four years of the group's existence, members addressed and reflected on topics appropriate to their stage of spiritual and educational development. In the first year, most of the groups focused on the topic, "Who I am and what I believe." Each group member had one meeting to tell his story in relation to that assigned topic. The two facilitators were generally the first to share their stories during this initial year and thereby attempted to model the process, and the skill and depth with which they did this usually set the tone for how the younger men in the group told their stories. This first-year topic usually served as an effective vehicle for individuals to learn to become comfortable with self-disclosure in as deep a level as the individual participants were able to reach at this point in their lives, and many acknowledged that they had been able to talk about issues that they had never before talked about with other people or in other settings.

In the second year, many, but not all, of the groups focused on the topic of relationships. Using the same storytelling format of one man per session, each member reflected on the most important relationships in his life, which for many young men brought to the fore especially their relationship with their fathers. Others focused on other relationships, or other relationships in addition to their relationship with their fathers, as they explored their connections with their mothers, siblings, or significant others. Sometimes a young man who had grown up without a father actively involved in his life explored what this had meant for him, perhaps including the discomfort he may have had in interacting with other men. A young man telling his story may have explored the ways in which his beliefs and self-understanding had influenced his relationships and how his relationships had influenced his beliefs. The disclosure of the nature and quality of relationships with father, mother, and other significant others, including oneself, allowed men to dig deeper into who they are. This is a significant subject to explore for many traditional-age college men at this point in their development because their relationships with both their family and their peers are often in transition.

The third year was the most challenging for many of the spirituality groups. One of the factors was that this was the year when many students studied abroad, and this diminished the size and diversity of the membership of the groups for those who remained on campus. Some of the groups combined with each other, moving back into their original groups the following year. Others attempted to maintain some type of ongoing contact with members who were abroad. In addition, there was no consensus about what topic was most appropriate for men at this stage of their personal and academic development. Some groups took up the theme of "authenticity" during their third year. In this case, authenticity was construed as meaning how one is appropriately transparent about his values and beliefs, and students usually told stories that revealed how their internal selves and their public selves did or did not coincide. Other groups devoted year three to the topic of beauty. This often led to important discussions about what makes someone beautiful or what it meant to say that a man is beautiful, and the men told stories to illustrate how they understood beauty in themselves and others. Still other groups attempted to go broader and deeper in discussing the topic of relationships they had explored the previous year. Whatever topic was discussed, this year allowed groups to go deeper into areas that were of most interest to the individual group. Cohesion and trust within the group had usually developed by this time, allowing for deeper exploration and a greater degree of comfortable self-disclosure than was present in previous years. This year's focus helped young men define more clearly their deepest values and the extent to which they had been able to express those values in their daily lives.

During their fourth year, almost all the groups attempted to allow each participant to articulate what he had learned through the group experience and to process how he anticipated that what he had learned would affect him in his postcollege life. Typically, members reflected on how the group process had changed over the years, as well as how they as individuals had changed. This year provided an opportunity for the participants to reflect on the entire process of the group, to take a brief look at how far they had traveled as individuals and as a group, and to look forward to how they anticipated that their experience in the group would influence them in the future. In some of the groups, students wrote brief essays summing up what their involvement in their group had meant to them, but this pattern did not become widespread. A few groups made plans to maintain a connection, such as forming a virtual group through e-mail to continue to keep in touch following graduation, but there has been no systematic assessment of how effective this has been.

ASSESSMENT OF THE PROGRAM'S EFFECTIVENESS

Shortly after the men's spirituality group program began, Mark Muesse, Professor of Religious Studies at Rhodes College, and Merle Longwood were asked to serve as outside, independent evaluators and consultants. In 1999, they began a series of annual visits to Saint John's to interview students, facilitators, and administrators to assess the effectiveness of the groups in helping students meet the university's mission to foster the intellectual and spiritual development of men. Drawing upon documents that had been developed in an attempt to articulate what the university sought to accomplish in providing an education for men, informed both by Benedictine values and by Muesse and Longwood's own work in men's studies, they sought to evaluate the program's success in five interrelated areas. Specifically, they wanted to know how the groups influenced participants' (1) self-understanding as men; (2) relationships with others outside the group, especially parents and other significant others; (3) sense of spirituality; (4) sense of justice and compassion; and (5) sense of vocation. Although there were certainly differences among the groups, it is possible to make some generalizations about the experiences of men in these groups.

1. *Self-Understanding as a Man.* Throughout all the groups, the men said that being a part of the group had helped them appreciate more fully what it means to be a man. They expressed gratitude for having been in a structured setting that allowed them to discuss issues that they would not otherwise discuss with other men. Frequently, men at every grade level commented that their closest friends were men outside the group, but that they had been able to discuss issues and problems in their lives more openly and honestly in their group than in any relationship they had outside the group. Many acknowledged that they had learned how to communicate about sensitive issues by the way the facilitators had modeled doing this. Members of first-year groups frequently said that it had been valuable to talk with other men about matters that were "deeper" than the usual conversations college men have about "sports or girls," and that through these conversations they had learned much about what it means to be a man in today's world. A member of a first-year group said that being in his group had made it possible for him for the first time to articulate what being a man meant to him, and he said this had definitely been a "self-realizing" experience. As the groups dis-

cussed aspects of the male role, the members helped each other develop their capacities for candidness and sensitivity, thus making it possible to "normalize" intimacy among men, as one member of a second-year group expressed it. Members of a third-year group indicated that when they were freshmen, they had been somewhat skeptical about joining an intensive, intentional all-male group, but that by the time they were juniors they "would not want it any other way." Members of the fourth-year groups elaborated most fully what they had learned through being a member of a group for all four years of their college experience, including the value of empathic "listening," the value of hearing and learning from other men's stories, and the importance of opening themselves up to a redefinition of masculinity (sometimes including adopting qualities they had previously regarded as "feminine"), to the point where they had come to view "masculinity" as a social construction to a large extent. Thus, the groups helped break down the cultural gender binds that encourage men to believe that being stereotypically masculine is the only authentic way to be a man.

2. *Life and Relationships outside the Group.* The men in all the groups characteristically observed that their involvement in their groups had a significant impact on their relationships outside the group. Having listened to other men in their group talk about their relationships had helped them develop insights about the dynamics of relationships and, consequently, they had become more self-conscious about the relationship issues present in their own lives. Many students commented that one of the most important benefits in being part of a group was that they had begun to understand their fathers in ways they had not before, as they had focused on this in their own stories as well as having listened to others talk about their relationships with their fathers. For many, this had led to an improved relationship with their fathers, including their newfound ability to talk with their fathers about issues they had never discussed before, and consequently they expressed gratitude that their relationships with their fathers had improved as a result of this increased awareness. Often, students presented what was almost a "textbook" version of the father-son relationship among middle-class European and European American males, as they explained how their fathers had provided them with the ideals of what they believed to be appropriate masculinity: being the provider, protector, disciplinarian in the family;

excelling at hunting, fishing, sports, and the outdoor life; being "concise" when speaking and "distant" when relating to the family. At the end of this account, the typical student also lamented not being as close to his father as he would like, while acknowledging the many ways he had become aware that he had been acquiring his father's ways of being masculine.

This usually elicited responses from group participants, who related experiences similar to the one offered by the initial story teller, confirming the prevalence of these ideals of masculinity among males of this social location. Occasionally, however, it brought out responses from men with different perspectives. One student, for example, who grew up in a fatherless home, talked about what it was like not to have a significant male figure during his formative years. He said his ideals of masculinity were gained from his older sisters. Although he believed his view of what it meant to be a man was not as confining as the "traditional" ideals experienced by fellow group members, he acknowledged that he found it easier to relate to females than to other males. Another young man explained how his inability to live up to the traditional masculine ideals—for example, being more interested in music than sports—had disappointed his father and had led his father to suspect him of being gay.

Others observed that their relationships with both parents and/or siblings had improved, as they themselves had learned to be more empathic and expressive within their families. On campus, they indicated that being in a group had helped them in their relationships with women as well as with other men. They perceived that the women on campus appreciated that they were involved in a spirituality group and that other "Johnnies" were often envious of their participation in a group. This envy was not always regarded as a positive development, especially by the facilitators, who wondered whether belonging to a spirituality group may have become a kind of status symbol among students, so that some first-year students, for example, might have joined a group more to impress their peers or to gain other benefits than because they were genuinely committed to the kind of serious inner work that the spirituality program endeavored to encourage. The observation by some facilitators that they struggled with high absenteeism and difficulties with scheduling seemed to underscore this point. Problems with attendance and scheduling were related to students' involvement in other activities across campus, but this also seemed to reflect less commitment to involvement in spirituality groups.

As the young men attained a high level of self-awareness and a critical understanding of how their lives had been shaped as males in American culture, they frequently agreed that conventional masculine roles were too confining and destructive to men and women, as they yearned for new definitions of what it means to be male. What seemed to be especially helpful about this aspect of the groups was that it allowed men to see that there are many ways to be a man. Hence, the groups helped break the cultural gender binds that encouraged men to believe that hegemonic masculinity is the only authentic form of manhood.

Often, the facilitators acknowledged how they themselves had experienced a further deepening in their own spiritual lives as they had shared personal stories with the members of the group, such as stories about their relationships with their dads. Many men indicated that being in a group had made them more comfortable in talking with others as individuals and as groups. A number of seniors described how their group had been particularly helpful as they dealt with particular situations and relationship issues that emerged during their four years together. In general, by the time they were seniors, the group members had attained a high level of self-awareness and a critical understanding of the ways in which their lives had been shaped as males in American culture. They all agreed that conventional masculine roles were too confining and often destructive to both men and women, and they yearned for new definitions for what it means to be male.

3. *Sense of Spirituality and Connection to God, the Universe, and Others.* Students grew in their ability to articulate the ways in which being involved in a group had impacted the members' spirituality. In a typical first-year group, a long pause occurred before anyone ventured to provide a response to a question related to this topic. Then, they often talked about what a "nice surprise" it was to discover that their facilitator monks were so accepting of them and that they were comfortable talking with them about their personal issues, including issues about their relationships with the women in their lives. They appreciated the monks' "different perspectives" and "unique insights." Although the freshmen spoke about spirituality mainly in the abstract, some were able to say that their concept of spirituality had been broadened as a result

of their group experience. A group that had participated in a weekend retreat said they had come to recognize that there was a connection between spirituality and sexuality, a relationship they had not previously recognized.

By the time they were seniors, most students were enthusiastic in discussing the importance the group had in the development of their spirituality. Participants agreed that the group was one of the few places—and for many, the only place—where they felt totally free to acknowledge their failures, mistakes, and inadequacies. As a safe place to share emotions and thoughts with others, the group was—by its very existence—a foil to some of the destructive aspects of conventional masculinity. One member said he believed the lessons he learned through his participation might help him avert a midlife crisis!

In all groups, the participants indicated how pleased they were to have been able to focus on spirituality, which they seemed to agree was quite different from institutional religion, although when they provided examples of their own spiritualities, they often used language that was quite conventionally religious. They described their groups as being religiously diverse, which was a positive assessment for them, although in actuality the diversity was usually different denominations of Christianity rather than including representation from different religions. Although the men emphasized that their groups had a wide variety of "spiritualities" within them, they more often focused on the similarities they discovered they had with each other. One individual who was a self-defined atheist described how he was grateful that he had been able to express this in his group, and he emphasized how his group had allowed each of its participants to articulate his own spirituality without any critical assessment by others in the group. He concluded from this that if one is comfortable with his own spirituality, then one is free to accept others' spiritualities, regardless of how different they may be from one's own. Other men said they were grateful that group members had supported them as they articulated their spiritualities that were not linked specifically to being involved in a church or other organized religious community. Many men noted that learning about the spirituality of others had helped them understand their own spiritual lives, and when they gave examples, they made reference to how others had discussed their experiences as well as their conceptions of the divine. Others indicated that it had been good for them to find out that others were also serious about wrestling with issues of faith. A number of men said, without providing many examples to illustrate it, that being part of the group had broadened their understanding of spirituality. One man said that his involvement in his group had enabled him to develop a more "integrated" understanding of spirituality. Another group member indicated that being a part of his group had led him to explore how to practice meditation.

It is interesting that the topic of "authenticity," the theme for many third-year groups, seemed to have been especially important for many group members in opening up their spirituality. The men frequently observed that they had appreciated learning about how the monks articulated their own spirituality, including the struggles they experienced in their faith journeys, so that they no longer viewed the monks totally as "the experts" whose lives were completely different from their own. As a result, even though they often remained wary about maintaining too close an identification with the Catholic Church, even if that was the religion in which they had been raised, they were able to appreciate the nuances within that tradition and to break down stereotypes they may have held about the monks as well as about the church of which the monks were exemplars. Very few of the men articulated their sense of spirituality having a relationship to "the universe," and this was probably a result of the structure of the group discussions, which encouraged them primarily to address spirituality in relation to the development of their inner lives and their interpersonal relationships.

The role of the monks was frequently commented upon by students in the groups. Several students reported that curiosity about the monks was one factor in their decision to participate in the groups. Several students indicated that during their involvement in a group, they had toyed with the idea of becoming a monastic, and at the very least, close relationships with the monks in the group generated a new respect for monastic life. Although in the early stages of group development, some of the students looked to the monks as "spirituality experts," this usually shifted over time, so it became more common for students to report their appreciation of the monks' humanity (especially the monks' candor in discussing their own sexuality) as they expressed a deepened interest in monastic life, both of which they would not have had apart from involvement in the spirituality groups. Some college men said that they appreciated very much the monks' willingness to express their religious doubts. This enabled the students to see the monks as more human and hence more endearing. One student said he rarely thought of the monks as "facilitators" any longer; now they were just fellow participants.

4. *Sense of Justice and Compassion for Others and the Earth.* Few of the men in any of the groups emphasized justice concerns beyond inter-personal relationships. The reticence to respond to this question may have been, in part, developmental in origin and, in part, cultural. In the United States, 18- and 19-year-olds are encouraged to focus more on immediate goals pertaining to their careers and education than on matters of social justice. In addition, it may be that other programs on the campus provided opportunities for them to be involved in activities oriented toward justice and care of the earth. It also seemed to be true that, as one third-year student commented, because the group he was in was very diverse politically, it tended to shy away from political issues that might have been disruptive, although he acknowledged that when such issues arose, the group was able to deal with them skillfully. In at least one of the groups, there were some who reflected on what it means to take care of the members of one's community and the ways in which their involvement in the group had given them deeper insights into how communities function. One group included a number of students who were involved in the "pink shirt" program on campus, a student-initiated program designed to overcome stereotypes of sexual minorities and others who did not conform to a dominant notion of masculinity on campus.

Members of another group discussed how they had experienced one of its members "coming out" as a gay man, and how important it had been for all of them to participate in this process respectfully as they incorporated this self-disclosure as a means of coming to appreciate diversity of sexual orientations, not as an abstract issue, but as a concrete reality. In this same group, it became clear that social justice concerns had been embodied in the group's dynamics, as conversations—often moving to vigorous debates—especially focused around two members of the group, one of whom was described by another student as the campus's "Mr. Social Justice" while the other was a self-described con-servative and a cadet in ROTC. These two young men had often taken opposite views on particular social and political issues and had been at the center of many lively group discussions. Both men said that despite their diametric viewpoints, they had each learned to respect the other's perspective and to respect each other as a person. Each of them reported having to revise misleading stereotypes about conservatives and liberals, respectively. It was also clear that the other members of the group benefited by observing that the opposing views between the two men did not disrupt their friendship. Men in other groups reported that their group's discussions and learning about the experience of some of the other members in their group had helped them become aware of social justice issues and how these issues had had a powerful impact on the lives of others, and as a result they had opened themselves up more in a way that made them more compassionate. Even though there are numerous aspects of the design of the campus and its programs that are oriented toward "care of the earth," only a few of the men indicated that they thought about "the earth" when they considered ways in which they might express justice and compassion.

5. *Sense of Vocation, Mission, or Purpose in Life—in relation to Family, Career, Church, or Community.* From 2001 onward, Muesse and Longwood added questions concerning vocation to help fulfill the university's administration of the Program for the Theological Exploration of Vocation, funded by the Lilly Endowment. In 2002, they proposed a series of vocational questions that were suggested to them by Diane Millis, director of the Lilly Endowment Planning Grant, College of Saint Benedict:

- What is the first thing that comes to mind when you hear the term "vocation"? What does "vocation" mean to you?

- To what extent have you experienced a sense of mission, purpose, or calling in your life?

- Which persons and/or what experiences have guided or shaped your understanding of your vocation?

- Have there been any barriers for you in either discovering or pursuing your vocation?

- What additional supports for discovering or developing your vocation are you seeking at this time?

As they returned to this topic in subsequent years, however, Muesse and Longwood compressed these questions into the briefer summary statement: Sense of Vocation, Mission, or Purpose in Life—in relation to Family, Career, Church, or Community. The answers given to questions about vocation, and other questions that students answered, contained some repetition, but it was valuable to single out the question of "vocation" to see how the group participants reflected on it when given an opportunity to focus on it specifically. Even first- and second-year students had quite sophisticated understandings of the concept of vocation. No student thought that vocation related exclusively to a priestly or other "religious" calling, and nearly all of them interpreted vocation as relating to something more than a job or career. One sophomore, however, defined vocation as one's "life's work, what makes you happy and benefits the world." Another said it was "everyone's role in the world." A first-year student said that vocation is "something God is calling you to do . . . It is more a lifestyle than an occupation." Perhaps the most sophisticated response was provided by a sophomore, who said that vocation is "embracing the universal call to holiness." First- and second-year students referred to the ways in which their involvement in the group had helped them to align their priorities in a proper way. Seniors emphasized the ways in which their development of life skills (listening without judgment, sharing, helping others) encouraged them to focus their lives, and one man who anticipated working with the homeless through a Catholic Charities program said that his involvement in the group had influenced his sense of vocation, particularly as he had chosen to work in this program because it would enable him to help other men. Several students said they felt a call to travel and work in another culture as a way to fulfill their vocations. One man said that his involvement in the group had helped him realize that becoming financially independent of his parents was an extremely important goal, at least an important aspect of vocation, in his life.

One of the models for vocational discernment that Muesse and Longwood discovered was that of Richard Bresnahan, Artist-in-Residence at Saint John's University, a potter who brings a visionary approach to his work. He salvages industrial waste products, does his firing of the kilns with deadfall, and maintains a broad range of environmentally sensitive practices that provide an important witness to the values of the Benedictine community that surrounds his work. He demonstrates how a man can live out an alternative form of masculinity—one that differs from the dominant norm of what it means to be a man—in his personal and family life as well as in his work. Although it was rare for students to refer to vocation in the traditional, narrow sense of a calling to a particular form of religious life, several of the young men acknowledged that they had, as a result of participating in a group, thought about the possibility of becoming a monastic. The men's close relationships with the monks who had been facilitators in their groups had clearly contributed to their developing a deep respect for monastic life.

Although most of the men, at various stages in their college careers, articulated refined notions *about* vocation, almost all of them believed that they had not yet discovered their personal vocations. Lack of experience seemed to be the greatest hindrance to vocational discernment at this point in their lives. One student suggested, rather profoundly, that vocation may in fact be a retrospective judgment. Only as one looks back at his or her life can one truly say, "That was my vocation." Perhaps the most poignant comment was made was by a senior, anticipating he would begin a tour of duty in the army following graduation, which he regarded as a call to service, who said that he realized the question he would have to answer was a profound moral one: "Can I kill someone?"

CONCLUDING COMMENTS

We have described the multidimensional ways in which Saint John's University has sought to engage college men as men. By engaging questions of gender and masculinity in the curriculum, and even more extensively in extracurricular programming and resident life, the university has, in the words of Michael Kimmel, become not just an institution of higher learning *of* men, with programming administered *by* men, but it has become a college *for* men, as it helps men reflect on the implications of gender in all aspects of their lives.[30] In assessing the effectiveness of the groups in helping students meet the university's mission to foster the intellectual and spiritual development of men, Muesse and Longwood concluded that one of the most significant dimensions that contributed to that transformation was the men's spirituality program.

30. Michael Kimmel, "Afterward," in *Developing Effective Programs and Services for College Men*, New Directions for Student Services, vol. 107, ed. Gar E. Kellom (San Francisco: Jossey-Bass, 2004) 97–100.

The group experience had been highly successful in assisting these young men in challenging masculine stereotypes as they learned more reflectively authentic ways to be a man in our society today; enriched their relationships with family, friends, and other significant people in their lives; deepened and broadened their spiritual development; and expanded their understanding of their vocations. Beyond its own campus, the spirituality program at Saint John's became an inspiration for a significant number of other institutions of higher learning to consider developing their own initiatives to enable college men to become more deeply engaged in exploring how they might connect more fully with the spiritual dimensions of their own lives and with other men, enabling them to become more integrated within themselves and in their relationships with others.

Using qualitative analysis, we will explore more fully in chapter 4 what this has meant on this campus and other campuses as we examine more precisely how the men who were interviewed understood "masculinity" and "spirituality." But before turning to that, a broader and historical perspective on how men have experienced spirituality in the United States needs to be provided.

3

American Men, Religion, and Spirituality

T̲O̲ ̲P̲R̲O̲V̲I̲D̲E̲ ̲P̲E̲R̲S̲P̲E̲C̲T̲I̲V̲E̲ ̲O̲N̲ how men in our country have related masculinity, religion, and spirituality, it will be helpful to understand how American men have dealt with these issues in the centuries that have preceded our own. Although we live in the twenty-first century, we carry with us the legacy of developments that occurred in the nineteenth century as a feminine or passive image of the church accompanied the changed relationship between church and state that occurred in secular society. This began with the changes in social, political, and economic processes brought about by the Industrial Revolution, as the church lost the protective relationship with established political power that it had held since Constantine. The church became increasingly domesticated, focused on the private sphere of home and family, as the traditional distinction between church and world evolved into a distinction between the home and the world, with matters related to the church located in the home, or private domestic sphere. Public society, on the other hand, lost its official relation to God or "the sacred" as the material world of politics and work became identified with the secular.[1]

Because the home was the sphere associated with women, the domestication of the church brought about a shift in the image of the feminine. Whereas women in classical Christianity had been regarded as "carnal" in contrast to men who represented spirituality and rationality, now women—especially white, economically privileged women—came

1. Rosemary Radford Ruether, *New Woman, New Earth: Sexist Ideologies and Human Liberation* (New York: Seabury, 1975) 76–77.

51

to be identified as more religious, more spiritual, more moral than men, though they continued to be viewed as irrational and emotional. The nineteenth-century Victorians privatized the spiritual realm as they placed women on a spiritual pedestal, shifting an earlier understanding of patriarchal dualism that had assumed men to be superior in spirit and reason while women were identified with the inferior aspects of body and emotion.[2] In the Victorian ideal, which found expression as "The Cult of True Womanhood" or "the cult of domesticity," "True Womanhood" incorporated four cardinal virtues—piety, purity, submissiveness, and domesticity—and religion or piety was the core of a woman's virtue and the source of her strength.[3]

As a result, the church—particularly the Protestant church—in the nineteenth century became a feminine preserve, and clergymen of that era increasingly bemoaned that their congregations were composed of a great disproportion of females. Howard Allen Bridgeman, a liberal Congregationalist, for example, writing in the Andover Review in 1890, posed the question dramatically: "Have We a Religion for Men?" Noting that "the women naturally gravitate to the prayer-meeting, and men as naturally to the penitentiary," he expressed his dismay that the gospel he preached appeared "limited by sex distinctions."[4] From the perspective of "real men" in the world of power and business, the appropriate role of the church was to serve the powerless—women and children—and they regarded the clergy with the perplexed contempt that a masculinist ethic reserves for the feminine. These men in the public sphere were upset or angered by clergy who "don't know their place" or who try to interfere in matters that they "know nothing about," such as the world of politics and economics.[5]

This discomfort among men in relation to religious matters brought about different responses. For example, two movements in

2. James B. Nelson, "Male Sexuality and the Fragile Planet: A Theological Reflection," in Redeeming Men: Religion and Masculinities, ed. Stephen B. Boyd, W. Merle Longwood, and Mark W. Muesse (Louisville, KY: Westminster John Knox, 1996) 273–4.

3. Barbara Welter, "The Cult of True Womanhood: 1820–1860," (1996). Online: http://www.pinzler.com/ushistory/cultwo.html.

4. Howard Allen Bridgeman, "Have We a Religion for Men," Andover Review 13 (1890) 388–96, quoted in Ann Douglas, The Feminization of American Culture (New York: Alfred A. Knopf, 1977) 98.

5. Ruether, New Woman, New Earth, 75ff.

the late Victorian period—the Freethinkers and the Men and Religion Forward Movement (M&RFM)—gave dramatically contrasting answers to the question: "Is it manly to be Christian?"[6] The most fully articulated negative response to the question was given by an organized movement of atheists known as Freethought. The Freethinkers movement attracted thousands of middle-class, European American, heterosexual men who formed local, state, and national groups, of which the most important were the Free Religious Association and the National Liberal League, subsequently renamed the American Secular Union. They organized secular churches that met weekly to sing, listen to lectures, and attend Sunday school. They published books and periodicals, including *The Boston Investigator, The Index,* and *The Truth Seeker.* They founded the town of Liberal, Missouri and the Liberal University in Silverton, Oregon.

Perceiving the church as "feminized," dominated by women and therefore weak, sentimental, and irrational, Freethinkers argued that atheism was more appropriate for men because it provided a more manly option than did Christianity and because religious belief tended to make men sentimental, weak, and "soft-minded." Therefore, men could realize authentic masculinity only by rejecting Christianity. Having cast off the shackles of Christian belief, the Freethinking man could embrace a form of atheistic manhood that was characterized by "masterliness," which encouraged the bold exercise of reason, unfettered by superstition and a servile subjection to religious dogma.[7] For such a man, Christian belief was antithetical to manhood. Atheism, then, was the only manly option.

The M&RFM of 1911–1912 took the opposite position. Men in this movement contended that authentic Christianity, in contrast to its feminized form dominant in their day, was essentially "masculine, militant, [and] warlike." A sympathetic observer of the movement commented at the time the movement was emerging: "For some time past it has been noted in the United States that the Churches are falling more and more into the hands of women. They say that on average there are three women Church members to one male. To arrest this tendency and to

6. This discussion draws heavily from Evelyn A. Kirkley, "Is It Manly to Be Christian? The Debate in Victorian and Modern America," in *Redeeming Men: Religion and Masculinities,* ed. Stephen B. Boyd, W. Merle Longwood, and Mark W. Muesse (Louisville, KY: Westminster John Knox, 1996) 80–88.

7. Kirkley, "Is It Manly to Be Christian?" 81.

restore the requisite masculine element to popular religion in the States, a syndicate was formed for the purposes of uniting evangelical Churches in America and of combining efforts to bring men and boys into the Church."[8]

Men in the M&RFM believed that the promotion of this authentic interpretation of religion would produce more true Christian men, ready for "a heroic life of consecration and sacrifice." In turn, they believed that these more authentically masculine men would save the church from effeminacy and have a better chance of winning the world to Christ. This movement, which brought business methods into the practice of religion, attracted men from a wide diversity of Protestant denominations—mostly evangelical churches—and held forums, conferences, and public religious meetings in all the major cities, in places such as Carnegie Hall in New York City, and many small towns across the United States. It frequently featured well-known speakers at its events, including, for example, President Taft, who was among the speakers at a meeting on "The World's Peace" in Carnegie Hall in New York City in April, 1912. The movement was endorsed by prominent Protestants such as William Jennings Bryan, Washington Gladden, Harry Emerson Fosdick, John Mott, Josiah Strong, Booker T. Washington, and Jane Addams.[9]

The M&RFM was a well-organized movement, and it used sophisticated marketing techniques, such as newspaper advertisements on sports pages and rented electronic billboards on Times Square, to reach out to men.[10] Its overarching slogan, "More Men for Religion, More Religion for Men," focused on six major areas: Bible study, boys' work, evangelism, social services, home and foreign missions, and interchurch work. Although the M&RFM drew upon the revivalist impulses that had been developing within Protestantism during the late nineteenth century, its appeal to Christian service was the focus that most effectively

8. W. T. Stead, *The Review of Reviews*, April, 1912, reprinted at the W. T. Stead Resources Site, http://www.attackingthedevil.co.uk/reviews/forward.php.

9. Michael A. Longinow, "The Price of Admission? Promise Keepers' Roots in Revivalism and the Emergence of Middle Class Language and Appeal in Men's Movements," in *The Promise Keepers: Essays on Masculinity and Christianity*, ed. Dane S. Claussen (Jefferson, NC: McFarland, 2000), 50; Kirkley, "Is It Manly to Be Christian?" 83.

10. Ibid.

drew men into the movement. Walter Rauschenbush claimed that this movement had "made social Christianity orthodox."[11]

Both groups viewed the relationship between masculinity and Christianity as critical. The Freethinkers repudiated Christianity in the name of true manliness, while the M&RFM embraced it, for the M&RFM men were by nature active, aggressive, and oriented to the business efficiency that made for industrial growth. Leaders in this movement encouraged men to pay more attention to their families and to work toward Christianizing the economic order in order to create a context within which the message of individual salvation could be promulgated. It was akin to the Social Gospel movement, as its "primary goal was to educate Christians about social conditions in their own communities and to inspire and equip them to improve these conditions."[12] This work required strong men who were well organized, on the model of a good business, parallel to the view of Charles Sheldon's 1897 novel, *In His Steps: What Would Jesus Do?*, which portrayed Jesus as an astute businessman. Men were to be God's partners in a heavenly corporation.[13] The M&RFM caught the attention of a lot of men during its seven months of existence, but it did not have staying power.

More enduring than the M&RFM was a phenomenon that emerged in the middle of the nineteenth century that came to known as "Muscular Christianity," a movement oriented "to bring manliness in its various manifestations to church, and to keep it awake when it got there."[14] The term Muscular Christianity had its origin in a review of Charles Kingsley's novel, *Two Years Ago*, published in Britain in 1857.[15] The term

11. Gail Bederman, "The Women Have Had the Charge of the Church Work Long Enough: The Men and Religion Forward Movement of 1911–1912 and the Masculinization of Middle-Class Protestantism, *American Quarterly* 41 (September 1989) 456, quoted in Longinow, "The Price of Admission," 51.

12. Gary Scott Smith, "Men and Religion Forward Movement of 1911–1912: New Perspectives on Evangelical Social Concern and the Relationship between Christianity and Progressivism," *Westminster Theological Journal* 49 (1987) 107, quoted by Dane S. Claussen, "What the Media Missed about the Promise Keepers," in *Standing on the Promises: The Promise Keepers and the Revival of Manhood*, ed. Dane S. Claussen (Cleveland: Pilgrim, 1999) 23.

13. Kirkley, "Is It Manly to Be Christian?" 83.

14. Norman Vance, *The Sinews of the Spirit: The Ideal of Christian Manliness in Victorian Literature and Religious Thought* (Cambridge: Cambridge University Press, 1985) 29.

15. Randy Balmer, "Introduction," in *The Promise Keepers*, ed. Dane S. Claussen (Jefferson, NC: McFarland, 2000) 3.

was pejorative, as the reviewer criticized the author's celebration of heroic Christian activity, but the term gained popularity as it became associated with a variety of attempts to emphasize masculine expressions of piety and, with other initiatives, to celebrate a combination of robust physical manliness with a call to Christian service. Often employing the language of sports and athletics, Muscular Christianity sought to rescue the image of Jesus from the effeminate portrayals of Jesus prevalent at that time, in its efforts to remasculinize the church.

Muscular Christianity's best-known spokesman was Billy Sunday, who emerged at the turn of the twentieth century, taunting male audiences to become "real men," to "hit the saw dust trail," and to give their lives to Jesus. Formerly a well-paid professional baseball player who played right fielder consecutively for the Chicago, Pittsburgh, and Philadelphia baseball teams, Sunday was converted by the street preaching of Harry Monroe of the Pacific Garden Mission in Chicago.[16] He became a much less well-paid evangelist with the previously evangelistic YMCA. A strong, sinewy athletic man, he injected his boundless energy into his rousing sermons. He repudiated the idea that a Christian has to be a "sort of a dishrag proposition, a wishy-washy sissified sort of galoot that lets everyone make a doormat out of him." Sunday proclaimed. "Let me tell you, the manliest man is the man who will acknowledge Jesus Christ."[17] Sunday's goal was to transform feminized religion and "get into the world . . . to strike the death blow at the idea that being a Christian takes a man out of the busy whirl of the world's life and activity and makes him a spineless, effeminate proposition."[18]

That the question of which was the more "manly"—atheism or Christianity—was even a matter of debate demonstrates both the unease that men in our country often have with religion and their anxieties about their own masculinity. In the twenty-first century, there is evidence that this uneasiness remains current. One of the popular slogans of Promise Keepers, the evangelical men's movement, is "Real Men Love Jesus." If men were truly comfortable with loving Jesus, asserting that

16. William G. McLoughlin Jr., *Billy Sunday Was His Real Name* (Chicago: University of Chicago Press, 1955) 6.

17. Quote by Sunday cited in McLoughlin, *Billy Sunday,* 179.

18. Quote by Sunday cited in McLoughlin, *Billy Sunday,* 141. See also Roger A. Bruns, *Preacher: Billy Sunday and Big-Time American Evangelism* (New York: W. W. Norton, 1992).

this is something real men do would not be necessary. It is hard to imagine a corresponding motto "Real Women Love Jesus."

Given this history, one need not look far to understand why men in the United States are ambivalent about religion. The ideals of masculinity encourage men to be independent, self-sufficient, rational, active, controlling, emotionally restrictive, and competitive. Of course, not all men live up to these ideals, but they are the basic standards by which one's masculinity is frequently judged. This came to light in a special way to co-author Merle Longwood, who recently invited into one of his classes a young woman who is transforming her gender identity to become a "transman." He (this person's preferred pronoun) expressed his ambivalence about having some of these "masculine" qualities affirmed by others now that he is in the process of changing his gender, while the same qualities had been criticized when he exhibited them as a lesbian woman.

On the other hand, spirituality and religion often advocate qualities that are at odds with these dominant masculine values. Spirituality, in spite of Billy Sunday's efforts to the contrary, usually tends to value interiority, yielding, cooperation, connectedness, emotionality, and community. It is little wonder that despite the dominance of men in leadership positions, many more women than men participate in religious institutions in the United States. Religiously active men, even those in leadership, are often regarded with suspicion by other men, almost as if they constitute a third gender. Theologian James Nelson recalls seeing the restrooms in a Swedish church designated for "women," "men," and "clergy."[19]

By American standards of conventional masculinity, the manliness of religious men, especially overtly religious men, may be in doubt. We find this manifested in the way in which Promise Keepers, to which we will turn our attention next, conducted its rallies, while it was reaching its peak, in the most masculine of venues: the football stadium.

---

19. James B. Nelson, personal communication with Merle Longwood and Mark Muesse (April, 1995).

PROMISE KEEPERS AND THE MYTHOPOETIC MEN'S MOVEMENT: LATE TWENTIETH-CENTURY ATTEMPTS TO AFFIRM MEN'S SPIRITUALITY

Acknowledging that there was not one but several men's movements that emerged in the 1970s and 1980s, Kenneth Clatterbaugh identified eight perspectives to explain the stirrings of North American men that result-ed in diverse movements: the conservative perspective, the profeminist perspective, the men's rights perspective, the mythopoetic perspective, the socialist perspective, gay male perspectives, African American men's perspectives, and the evangelical Christian men's movement.[20] The most significant movements for understanding what happened to men and religion in the United States in the latter part of the twentieth century are Promise Keepers, identified by Clatterbaugh as the evangelical Christian men's movement, and the mythopoetic men's movement. Because they came into existence almost simultaneously, we will discuss these two phenomena together as we examine their similarities and ponder their differences.[21]

Looking at their shared features, both are, first and foremost, movements that are explicitly *religious* or *spiritual* movements. That is, both the mythopoetic movement and Promise Keepers are fundamen-tally religious or spiritual in nature and not, in essence, covert political movements or antifeminist backlashes.

Second, it is important to note that both movements draw from a similar constituency, but upon closer examination, there appears to be almost no overlap between the movements in terms of participation or leadership. Although both the Promise Keepers and the mythopo-etic movement share common demographics, the participants in each movement come from essentially different worlds.

---

20. Kenneth Clatterbaugh, *Contemporary Perspectives on Masculinity: Men, Women, and Politics in Modern Society*, 2nd ed. (Boulder: Westview, 1997).

21. This section on Promise Keepers and the mythopoetic men's movement draws significantly from an unpublished paper, "Religion and American Men at the End of the Twentieth Century: A Comparative Analysis of Men's Spiritual Movements," by Merle Longwood and Mark Muesse, presented at the annual conference of the American Men's Studies Association (AMSA), held at Buffalo, New York in March, 2000. In *Politics of Masculinities: Men in Movements* (Thousand Oaks, CA: Sage, 1997), Michael A. Messner discusses these two movements together in a chapter, "Essentialist Retreats: The Mythopoetic Men's Movement and the Christian Promise Keepers" (pp. 16–35).

Third, both of these men's movements have been subjected to intense interest by the media and the larger culture. They are, in addition, frequently criticized by feminists, profeminists, and others who find them to be at best curious, and at worst, downright dangerous.

Fourth, both movements have had meteoric careers. They began with initial enthusiasm and saw significant early growth, then peaked after several years and began to decline. Although neither movement has totally disappeared, both have significantly diminished from their heydays. Neither movement, comparable to what happened to men's movements in the early twentieth century and in contrast to the women's movement, has evidenced much staying power.

These prima facie resemblances spur us to compare these movements more critically, especially as we examine the rise and decline of these movements. We may question whether their appearances late in the twentieth century intimate enduring concerns within men about religion or spirituality, concerns that have not been sufficiently recognized or addressed. We may ponder why each of these movements began to decline after a brief career and ask what this suggests about future men's movements. It will be helpful to discuss each of these movements in terms of its constituency, organizational structure and leadership, ideology, and decline.

Constituency

The mythopoetic movement is rather fluid in nature, so it is difficult to establish a demographic profile of its participants based on solid empirical data. But it is possible to describe, with some accuracy, the general characteristics of mythopoetic men based on personal observations and the observations of others. Michael Schwalbe, who has written the most substantial empirical study of this movement, estimated that at its peak (ca. 1992), as many as 100,000 American men had participated in some kind of mythopoetic event.[22] At the time of his writing, Schwalbe suggested that the number of regular, committed participants was probably much smaller. The vast majority of mythopoetic participants in the United States are European American, with a significant but considerably smaller representation of African American men. While in the movement's early years there were intense efforts to bring a larger

22. Michael Schwalbe, *Unlocking the Iron Cage: The Men's Movement, Gender Politics, and American Culture* (New York: Oxford University Press, 1996) 4.

number of African American men into the movement, mythopoetics simply did not have the same appeal to blacks as it did among whites. Most mythopoetic men are middle-class to upper middle-class, though many of them grew up in working-class homes. Most are well educated, the majority having attended college, and many have advanced degrees. Typical members are between 35 and 60 years old.[23] Rarely do younger men participate in mythopoetic events.

Beyond these demographic data, it is possible to characterize mythopoetic participants in terms of some psychological and emotional factors. Many mythopoetic men reported that their fathers were emotionally distant and/or physically absent during their childhood years. Consequently, many mythopoetic men rejected their father's masculinity and have come to believe that there is something bad about men as such.[24] They tend, therefore, to have closer relationships with women than with men, whom they frequently see as competitive and threatening. Accordingly, many mythopoetic men disdain competitive practices and philosophies and often find themselves sympathetic to feminist criticisms directed at macho men. Finally, a very large number of mythopoetic men are involved in some kind of twelve-step or recovery group and have experienced a major trauma such as divorce, loss of job, or substance addiction in their adult lives.[25]

Like the mythopoetic men's movement, participants in Promise Keepers events, especially those who have attended the mass conferences that have characterized this movement, are middle-aged and middle-class. Though we need more systematic studies to confirm the data, a poll taken by the *Washington Post* of participants who attended the Stand in the Gap Assembly on the National Mall in Washington, DC in 1997 revealed that 80 percent of the men identified themselves as white, 14 percent as black, and 2 percent as Asian, while 4 percent said Other or refused to answer that question. (By contrast, the speakers for that gathering, as well as the regional conferences in those years, had a carefully constructed balance that included prominent religious leaders from the African American, Latino, Native American, and Asian American communities.) Most were middle-aged, with 75 percent between the ages of 30 and 60, but there was a substantial minority

23. Ibid., 19.
24. Ibid., 19–20.
25. Ibid., 22–23.

of younger men, which differentiates Promise Keepers to some extent from the mythopoetic movement. Seventy-six percent had attended some college, were college graduates, or had completed a postgraduate course of study. The majority had family incomes between $30,000 and $75,000 per annum. The *Post*'s survey discovered that the attendees at the Washington mall event said their number one problem (for 62 percent of the men) was sexual sin.[26]

Structure and Leadership

The mythopoetic men's movement is highly decentralized and has little national organization. Consequently, there is no official spokesperson or figurehead for mythopoetic men.[27] It is true that the poet Robert Bly is often credited with initiating this movement and is often called its "grandfather," but Bly's role as leader has been generally exaggerated. In the 1980s and 1990s, mythopoetic "leaders" such as Bly, Jungian psychologist James Hillman, storyteller Michael Meade, and theologian Robert Moore inspired mythopoetic men through their writings and occasional appearances at weekend events, but in no sense have they ever wielded organizational clout or spoken for the movement as a whole. Mythopoetics is far more a grassroots movement, with the most significant organization and events based at the local level in municipal men's councils, men's centers, and smaller, less formal men's support groups. The closest thing to a national organization was groups such as the New Warrior Network, later renamed the ManKind Project, which sponsored weekend initiation events throughout the United States, and similar groups on regional levels. The movement attempted to maintain national periodicals such as *Wingspan* and *Man!*, but after several years of struggling, these publications finally folded for financial reasons.

In contrast to the mythopoetic movement, Promise Keepers is highly centralized, and its founder, former University of Colorado football coach Bill McCartney, has played a central role in its leadership since the movement began as a local fellowship of men focusing on prayer, fasting, and mutual encouragement, but it grew into an organization that sponsored many annual stadium-based conferences for men, featuring multiple speakers and state-of-the-art technology. At its peak,

26. Richard Morin and Scott Wilson, "Men Were Driven to 'Confess Their Sins,'" *Washington Post*, October 5, 1997, A1, A19.

27. Schwalbe, *Unlocking the Iron Cage*, 5–6.

in 1997, it was a highly successful corporation with headquarters in Denver, a budget of $117 million ($9 million to $10 million allocated for the national Washington rally), and a staff of 363 employees.[28] A good part of its budget came from stadium rallies, which generally charged its participants $60 apiece to attend a conference.

Much less information is available about the small local fellowships that Promise Keepers attempted to make the foundation of the organization, and these cell groups have received little attention from most of the movement's interpreters, who have focused almost exclusively on the rallies. Promise Keepers had once claimed that its large conferences would be discontinued once the movement was firmly established at the local level, but it does not seem that the organization has supported local efforts sufficiently well to make that possible.

Ideology: Spirituality

The mythopoetic movement and Promise Keepers are fundamentally religious or spiritual in nature, but they differ in how they construe this. Their efforts are to claim, valorize, and develop spirituality for men. Although both movements attempt to do this in very different—and perhaps even mutually exclusive—ways, it is important to note this common purpose because it signals implicit resistance to certain elements of hegemonic masculinity.[29] In short, both Promise Keepers and the mythopoetic movement oppose the notion that it is unmanly to be spiritual. Spirituality and religion, which have been regarded as femi-

---

28. Gustav Niebuhr, "Religious Rally in Capital Is a Test of Faith," *New York Times*, October 3, 1997, A1, A10.

29. The term hegemonic masculinity was introduced by R. W. Connell to refer to the normative ideal of masculinity, the most socially endorsed form of masculinity within the gender hierarchy of our culture. As the term is used by scholars of men's studies, it has come to denote ideals appropriate for European American, educated, middle- or upper-class, heterosexual, culturally Christian males. Nonhegemonic masculinity, in contrast, is a socially constructed notion of ideals appropriate for those outside this group: poor and lower-class men; Native American, African American, Asian American, Hispanic, and Jewish men, as well as gay men. See Stephen B. Boyd, W. Merle Longwood, and Mark W. Muesse, "Preface," in *Redeeming Men*, ed. Boyd, Longwood, and Muesse, xv. For a more detailed discussion of this concept, see R. W. Connell, *Gender and Power: Society, the Person, and Sexual Politics* (Stanford, CA: Stanford University Press, 1987) 183–6. An updated discussion of this concept has been provided by R. W. Connell and James W. Messerschmidt in "Hegemonic Masculinity: Rethinking the Concept," *Gender & Society* 19.6 (December 2005) 829–59.

nine domains from the nineteenth century onward, are now heralded as appropriate to men. For this reason, mythopoetics and Promise Keepers tend to exaggerate other elements of hegemonic masculinity to provide a greater comfort in appropriating aspects of femininity.

Most mythopoetic men would spurn the label "religious" for their movement but would easily embrace the term "spiritual." With this distinction, mythopoetic men endeavor to affirm the movement's intent to develop men's interior, personal lives and to distance themselves from the institutional religion of churches and synagogues. Traditional, organized religion embodies too much of what mythopoetic men find problematic in their own lives and in the world: hierarchies of power and authority; doctrinal dogmatism; emotional, physical, and sexual restriction; the tendency to be judgmental; categories of do's and don'ts. Yet much of the form of religion, they believe, is worth keeping, such as ritual, mythology, chanting and drumming, prayer and meditation, compassion for others and the earth, and a sense of purpose and mission. Clearly, mythopoetic men find the arational elements (not grounded in rationality but not necessarily irrational) of traditional religion to be more compelling than theology, creeds, and polity—religion's more systematic dimensions.

It is significant, however, that although mythopoetic men find the forms of ritual and mythology meaningful, they do not widely embrace the ritual and myths of Christianity or Judaism. In part, this may be due to a troubling feature of the central Christian myth: the suffering of an innocent Son to satisfy a Father's wrath. Perhaps mythopoetic men who have experienced their own fathers as distant or abusive are made subconsciously uncomfortable by this tale. Many mythopoetic men prefer to use the Native American metaphor "Grandfather" rather than "Father" to refer to the divine.[30]

Instead, they turn to premodern and nonwestern traditions for spiritual inspiration. Thus, they appropriate sweat lodges and talking councils from Native Americans, European fairy tales such as "Iron John," meditation from Eastern religions, and the poetry of Rumi and Kabir.[31] But equally important is the framework of Jungian psychology, which provides a quasi-religious philosophy with deep affinities for

---

30. See Matthew Fox, *The Hidden Spirituality of Men: Ten Metaphors to Awaken the Sacred* (Novato, CA: New World Library, 2008).

31. Schwalbe, *Unlocking the Iron Cage*, 47–48.

imagery, symbolism, myths, and rituals. Jungianism provides a lingua franca for mythopoetic men, a language to understand and shape their experiences, to bring together their interior lives with the myths and rituals they seek to appropriate.[32]

In contrast to mythopoetic men, Promise Keepers affirm their identity as Christians, as they embrace the Bible as the source of their basic teachings and incorporate a mix of traditional hymns (though often in contemporary tempos) and more contemporary songs in their gatherings. Promise Keepers emerged within the context of more broadly based developments in evangelical and pentecostal-charismatic Christianity.[33] Indeed, Promise Keepers is a personalist revival movement that is involved in the delicate task of building a big-tent coalition among these related but distinguishable movements in conservative Christianity as well as a sizeable component of mainstream Protestants and even some Roman Catholics.[34]

Having said that, it is interesting to note that in the *Washington Post* survey of Promise Keepers rally participants, 90 percent of the men answered "yes" when asked if they were born-again evangelical or charismatic Christians. Even so, two out of three said they had "drifted away from their religious faith" at some time, and one out of five said they held "intolerant views of another race." One in five admitted to having "committed a sexual sin while married," and one in four said he had battled alcohol or drugs. In response to a question about the single biggest reason they came to Washington, one in four men said "to show unity with other Christian men."[35] Promise Keepers has tapped into this reservoir of need among men to identify with religion and with each other, and they have found a clever way to deal with it—in a sports event atmosphere. A call for a remasculinized image of Jesus and a call for men to assume leadership roles in their families are widely promulgated among Promise Keepers. Numerous creative rituals, but not those associated with traditional Christianity such as sharing the Eucharist, are built into Promise Keepers events. And the altar calls, an important high point in each Promise Keepers conference, are organized by lead-

---

32. Ibid., 213–27.

33. See Merle Longwood, "Standing on the Promises and the Broader Conversation," in *Standing on the Promises*, ed. Dane S. Claussen (Cleveland: Pilgrim, 1999) 1–2.

34. Ibid.

35. Morin and Wilson, "Men Were Driven," A1, A19.

ers to make those who respond feel as though they are going through a masculine rite of passage. Christianity is like a team or an army into which one is initiated, with Jesus as the coach or commander. Echoing in some ways the Muscular Christianity movement aimed at men at the turn of the twentieth century, Promise Keepers encourages men to stand up and be real men and give their hearts to Jesus. Billy Sunday's message has thus found an echo at Promise Keepers rallies, where scores of men wear T-shirts emblazoned with numerous slogans, such as the theme of a given year's conferences, or "Bikers for Jesus."

Ideology: Gender Perspectives

Both the Promise Keepers and the mythopoetic men's movement were men-only affairs in the past, and for this, great suspicion was cast on both movements by those on the outside. Many saw this sexual exclusivism as just another manifestation of the "boys' club" and an effort to reinscribe patriarchy in the face of the progress of women in the past several decades. It is possible, however, to put this "male only" dimension in a different light. Promise Keepers and the mythopoetic movement began as efforts to reclaim spirituality for men, over against the masculine ideal that regarded spirituality as unmanly. But to go against the ideal of masculinity in this society is risky business. Men who fail to conform to these standards often find themselves ridiculed, ostracized, and even physically abused. One of the functions of excluding women from these gatherings was to make it possible for men to engage in feminine behaviors—crying, grieving, embracing, and turning inward—in a safe environment, without fear of reprisal.

In the mythopoetic movement, the desire to be spiritual and yet manly is also a factor in the way the group understands the nature of gender and the relationships between the sexes. The mythopoetic movement tends to regard gender as biological realities, "hardwired" (to use Robert Moore's terminology)[36] into the psyches of men and women. This gender essentialism is consistent with the Jungian philosophy undergirding the movement. Mythopoetic men thus speak of the need to recover "deep masculinity," to distinguish what they regard as genuine or mature masculinity from the problematic "toxic" masculinity of

---

36. Schwalbe, *Unlocking the Iron Cage*, 249 n. 11.

immature males.[37] The problem with men, they maintain, is not masculinity per se, but immature, shallow masculinity. The solution for men wanting to recover their spiritual dimensions is to engage deep masculinity, available to them through certain archetypal images (king, warrior, magician, and lover).[38] Only other men—particularly, other men who have been initiated into genuine manhood—can assist with accessing the deep masculine. This is one reason that men involved in mythopoetic activities do not allow women on the premises.

"Deep masculinity," interestingly, comprises qualities commonly regarded as feminine: nurturing and caregiving, emotional expression, spiritual connection, the appreciation of relationships and community, and awareness of the body. But the mythopoetic insistence that these traits, along with more traditionally masculine ones, be considered part of genuine masculinity reveals the anxiety about appearing manly. Part of that anxiety, undoubtedly, derives from the fact that mythopoetic men have to deviate from the ideals of hegemonic masculinity to develop their spiritual natures.

In the past, Promise Keepers has also organized their events for "men only," to enable men to be spiritual and manly. One of the clearest interpretations of how Promise Keepers packed athletic stadiums with large numbers of men, with a mass outpouring of emotion resulting, is provided by John Stoltenberg, who reported an interview he had arranged with Glenn Wagner, at the time a vice president in charge of Promise Keepers' outreach to men in all the churches in the United States.[39] Stoltenberg asked Wagner why what happens at such gatherings could not happen if women were present. Wagner replied that there are "mixed signals" in our society about "what a man . . . there's this definition, that definition—get in touch with the feminine side, with Jungianism, be more sensitive yet strong—and the guy, he's absolutely confused. Yet in a context with just men, he is safe to discern what a man is, without anyone looking over his shoulder, without misperceived ideas." Stoltenberg pressed further, asking how this kind of gathering is different from other "men-only" gatherings where men do not feel

37. Ibid.

38. Robert Moore and Douglas Gillette, *King, Warrior, Magician, Lover: Rediscovering the Archetypes of the Mature Masculine* (New York: Random House, 1990).

39. John Stoltenberg, "Christianity, Feminism, and the Manhood Crisis," in *Standing on the Promises*, ed. Dane S. Claussen (Cleveland: Pilgrim, 1999) 89–110.

safe at all. Wagner responded that the difference was because of Promise Keepers' emphasis on worship, in which "there is more of abandonment to God taking place," and that within the context of worship, "the concerns about the guy sitting next to him are lessened." He concluded by saying that some men attend by themselves because they want anonymity, "but more often than not they leave with several new friendships, because they have come to a point where they're comfortable, where they can experience a nonsexual relationship with another man." Stoltenberg restated Wagner's point by commenting, "So you are saying that the depth of emotion that's released in that huge gathering couldn't happen with women and couldn't happen without God," to which Wagner responded, "Correct."[40] Later in his article, Stoltenberg commented on how he appreciated Promise Keepers' policy concerning homosexuality, which he was convinced would "head off intemperate and homophobic innuendoes at Promise Keeper stadium conferences" and send a "signal to all men in attendance at its events in sports arenas—venues typically athrob with homophobia—that as a matter of policy, Promise Keepers would not countenance gay-baiting."[41] This was, again, a return to the theme of how, in this setting, it would be possible to experience an intimate nonsexual relationship with another man.

Many Promise Keepers were torn by the social changes affecting women in general and their wives in particular, and their responses reflected this confusion. Of the Stand in the Gap attendees, 80 percent of the men were married and the overwhelming majority had children. Slightly more than half agreed that it would be better if the "man worked and the woman stayed at home with the children." But the majority of the married men with working wives said that their wives' employment "hardly ever" conflicted with their family lives. And 8 in 10 said that their wives worked, at least in part, because "she wants to work."[42] The leaders of Promise Keepers, for the most part, were quite unreceptive to feminist critiques of masculinity and men's institutional power, though they were aware of the number of problems that contemporary men share, and they frequently argued that these problems of today resulted from departures from men's natural roles, which they grounded in an

40. Ibid., 90.
41. Ibid., 103.
42. Morin and Wilson, "Men Were Driven," A1, A19.

essentialist reading of the Bible. It is not clear how closely the participants followed the leadership in their views of the roles of men and women.

Ideology: Politics

Both the mythopoetic movement and the Promise Keepers profess to be apolitical and are subjected to criticism for this claim. Some critics believe that Promise Keepers is a thinly disguised version of the Christian Coalition or the Moral Majority. Some think that both movements harbor implicit political agendas despite their proclamations to the contrary. Whatever the political intentions of these groups, both have attempted to distance themselves from the appearance of political partisanship.

In the case of the mythopoetic movement, the distancing effort arose as part of the basic intention of the movement: to allow individual men to feel personally empowered and comfortable with one another. Many followers believe that introducing partisan politics into mythopoetic events and groups would prove to be divisive and would ultimately take away the time and energy needed for the healing of men's psychic and emotional wounds.[43] Besides, politics is a nasty arena where men hurt other men and exercise abusive power. Men must first get their spiritual and psychological lives in order before attempting to address the larger issues of society and the political sphere.

Very rarely, however, do mythopoetic men consider that the very wounds they need to heal might have been caused by specific social and political dynamics, such as class and race. There is great resistance in the movement to thinking in social, political, and economic categories.[44] The Jungian underpinnings of mythopoetics, of course, greatly reinforce this tendency.

Promise Keepers insists that it does not have a political agenda and it interprets its goals in terms of individual transformation and the improvement of interpersonal relationships and dynamics within the family. But some profeminist men, many feminist women, and watchdog

43. See Edward Barton, ed., *Mythopoetic Perspectives of Men's Healing Work: An Anthology for Therapists and Others* (Westport, CT: Greenwood, 2000).

44. For a lively exchange of views involving profeminist men and mythopoetic men about these and other issues, see Michael S. Kimmel, ed., *The Politics of Manhood: Profeminist Men Respond to the Mythopoetic Men's Movement (and the Mythopoetic Leaders Answer)* (Philadelphia: Temple University Press, 1995).

organizations such as the Center for Democracy Studies view Promise Keepers as a movement with a not-so-subtle commitment to the reinscription of patriarchy, and they warn their followers of the movement's "ominous ties with fanatic right-wing organizations and their views on women, homosexuals, and non-Christians." In a widely read article in *The Nation*, Conason, Ross, and Cokorinos acknowledged that at Promise Keepers events and in Promise Keepers literature, "strident cultural messages are muted to the point of inaudibility." But, they concluded, "In conception and execution . . . Promise Keepers appears to be one of the most sophisticated creations of the religious right. It may come dressed in jeans and sound some themes reminiscent of the liberal left, but the movement lacks progressive content." They viewed Promise Keepers as the third wave of the conservative religious political movement, modernizing fundamentalism's public image. They concluded that by "mobilizing hundreds of thousands of men into a disciplined, hierarchical, national grass-roots formation with significant military connections but a subtle presentation, Promise Keepers poses a new challenge. Its promise may be our peril."[45]

Though we are as suspicious as these critics of the hierarchical view of the relationship between men and women that characterizes much of Promise Keepers teachings, we do not believe it is accurate to characterize Promise Keepers in right-wing political categories, whether such criticisms are put forward by the National Organization for Women or others on the political left. We are impressed by the delicate balancing that must be maintained to hold together the "big-tent coalition," a coalition that would be torn apart if Promise Keepers were to become involved in overt partisan political activism. Promise Keepers has deliberately not taken a stand on issues that are divisive in internal church politics, such as the ordination of women, and even abortion, although abortion has been discussed among the highest levels of the organization's leadership, and some of the movement's highly visible leaders have, in other contexts, been strongly identified with antiabortion politics. Furthermore, the leadership of Promise Keepers has explicitly denied

---

45. Joe Conason, Alfred Ross, and Lee Cokorinos, "The Promise Keepers Are Coming: The Third Wave of the Religious Right," *The Nation*, October 7, 1996, 11–12, 14, 16, 18–19. This parallels in many respects a special report prepared by Sterling Research Associates, *Promise Keepers: The Third Wave of the Religious Right* (New York: Sterling Research Associates, 1996).

any connection with the Christian Coalition, which has been overtly political and partisan.

Decline

There is no empirical documentation of the decline of the mythopoetic movement, but it is clear that the variety of activities that were widespread in the decade of the 1990s has largely dissipated in the United States. There is more empirical documentation available on the Promise Keepers' decline. It seems apparent that the appeal of both movements was in great part due to the way men were allowed and encouraged to set aside some aspects of their masculinity and embrace elements of femininity, all under the banner of being manly.

Promise Keepers, which grew exponentially during the early part of the 1990s, started in 1990 when University of Colorado football coach Bill McCartney developed a local fellowship of seventy-two men who sought to help each other become godly men. The next year, a regional gathering at the University of Colorado drew 4,200 men, followed by a conference that drew more than 22,000 in 1992 and one that brought out 50,000 in 1993. In 1994, the organization expanded its venues and more than 278,000 men came together in stadiums in six cities, and the numbers increased to 738,000 in thirteen cities in 1995. The peak years were in 1996, when 1.1 million men attended twenty-two stadium rallies, and 1997, when approximately 700,000 men attended the national Stand in the Gap event in Washington, DC[46] and an additional 639,000 men attended nineteen regional stadium conferences. For several years, a large number of clergy attended Promise Keepers conferences arranged especially for them in locations throughout the country. The numbers of participants attending stadium conferences has decreased since then. Promise Keepers reported that 450,000 men attended its nineteen conferences in 1998, 306,700 men in fifteen conferences in 1999, 195,000 men in sixteen conferences in 2000, 194,000 men in eighteen conferences in 2001, 176,000 men in sixteen conferences in 2002, 172,000 men in eighteen conferences in 2003, 179,000 men in eighteen conferences in 2004, an undisclosed number in twenty conferences in 2005, 132,000 men in eighteen conferences in 2006, 50,000 men in seven conferences

46. This was the number estimated by external crowd assessment experts. The Promise Keepers leadership continues to state that there were more than 1 million men in attendance.

in 2007, and 25,000 men in seven conferences in 2008.[47] Statistics about the number of conferences and numbers of attendees since 2008 are no longer published by Promise Keepers. There were seven conferences in five locations scheduled for 2010, and four types of events (Classic Events, Family Events, PK Road to Jerusalem, and PK Young Adult) planned for six locations in 2011.[48]

In 1997, at the Stand in the Gap Assembly, McCartney announced that the board of Promise Keepers had decided not to charge fees for forthcoming conferences, after downsizing its staff earlier that year and moving its headquarters to a more modest building on Pecos Street in Denver. The organization's official publication, *New Man*, was discontinued. The experiment in fee-less conferences had disastrous consequences, and in February 1998, the Promise Keepers announced that it would lay off its entire staff on March 31 and the organization would be run entirely by volunteers until donations and other income allowed the staff to be paid.[49] About $4 million in donations was received shortly after the announcement of layoffs and about 315 of the employees were rehired.[50] But through the remainder of 1998 and 1999, Promise Keepers continued to undergo restructuring and downsizing. Early in 2000, Promise Keepers announced it was closing its eight regional offices, so that all of its operations would be run from its headquarters in Denver,[51] and shortly afterwards the organization announced that it would again begin charging for its conferences—$69 for adults and $49 for youth under 18.[52] The 2008 gross income for the Promise Keepers was slightly less than $8 million,[53] or less than 7% of the budget at its peak in 1997.

47. Promise Keepers, "History of Promise Keepers." Online: http://www.promise keepers.org/about/pkhistory.

48. Promise Keepers Events. Online: http://www.promisekeepers.org/home/events2.

49. "Promise Keepers Group, Ailing Financially, to Quit Paying All 345 on Staff," *Washington Post*, February 20, 1998, A.03

50. AP, "Promise Keepers Brings Back Staff," *Boston Globe*, April 10, 1998, A.13.

51 AP, "Promise Keepers Closes Regional Offices," *Omaha World-Herald*, February 5, 2000, 62.

52. Mark A. Kellner, "Keeping Their Promises," *Christianity Today* 44.6 (May 22, 2000) 21.

53. Promise Keepers Financial Statement, IRS Form 990, 2008." Online: http://www.promisekeepers.org/uploads/su/_X/su_XlMsQYo5dCv2hAJxfDg/2008-Form-990-Public-Inspection-Copy.pdf.

Reasons for the decline in attendance at Promise Keepers events are not clear, but it may be because of the lack of new content and the limited value of the ritual for men who have attended more than one rally. As Mary Stewart van Leeuwen has suggested, "Like going to a Billy Graham crusade, once you've been to one PK rally you've pretty much been to all of them. The same sets of speakers appear at event after event, often giving much the same speeches."[54]

MAPPING RELIGION AND SPIRITUALITY IN THE TWENTIETH CENTURY

To set these developments related to men's efforts to express their religion or spirituality in the twentieth century in perspective, it will be helpful to place in a broader framework how religious attitudes and perspectives have changed in our nation's history. Martin E. Marty described three maps of earlier American religious history in addition to a new map that he regarded as reflecting the situation at the beginning of the last quarter of the twentieth century.[55] The first map depicted the world of 1492 to about 1776, representing the territorial and theological situations of colonial America. In nine of the thirteen colonies, one church had a near monopoly in its territory, and religion was established by law. Although not everyone practiced religion, the cultural norms were determined by the theological perspectives of the territories' elites. The second map, prominent in the nineteenth and early twentieth centuries, emerged out of and reflected denominational realities and the worldviews associated with them. Overlapping these two maps, a third showed the changes that had occurred by the middle of the twentieth century. Instead of emphasizing denominational identity, it emphasized norms that came from one "American Way of Life." It was best summarized by sociologist Will Herberg's *Protestant, Catholic, Jew,*[56] which argued that these three broad categories provided identifications and social locations for people whose strongest preoccupation was the American element in American

54. Mary Stewart van Leeuwen, "Mixed Messages on the Mall," *Christian Century* 114 (October 22, 1997) 932–34.

55. Martin E. Marty, *A Nation of Behavers* (Chicago: University of Chicago Press, 1976).

56. Will Herberg, *Protestant, Catholic, Jew: An Essay in American Religious Sociology* (Garden City, NY: Doubleday, 1955).

religion.[57] At the time of his writing, Marty suggested a more complex fourth map was taking form, which would emphasize group identity and social location that would encompass six clusters or zones: mainline religion, evangelicalism and fundamentalism, pentecostal-charismatic religion, the new religions, ethnic religion, and civil religion.[58] He acknowledged that some day there will be fifth or sixth maps.[59] More recently, borrowing a term from William James, "the habitual centres of energy," Marty has suggested a shift in the map, for he proposes that religious energies have sought channels that are quite different from the 1970s as they focus on

> the personal, private, and autonomous at the expense of the communal, the public, and the derivative; the accent on meaning at the expense of inherited patterns of belonging; concentration on the local and particular more than the cosmopolitan or ecumenical; concern for the practical and affective life accompanied by less devotion to the devotional and intellectual expressions; the feminist as opposed to the male dominated; and attention to separate causes more than to overarching civil commitments.[60]

Individuals "engage in expressions of individual autonomy over inherited authority . . . The individual seeker and chooser has come increasingly to be in control."[61]

The result, as sociologist Wade C. Roof suggests, is that "the current religious situation in the United States [is] characterized not so much by a loss of faith as a qualitative shift from unquestioned belief to a more open, questing mood. Underlying this, . . . a set of social and cultural transformations have [*sic*] created a quest culture, a search for certainty, but also the hope for a more authentic, intrinsically satisfying life."[62] As a consequence, a "spiritual marketplace" has developed, in which religious or spiritual "suppliers" provide, outside of established religious organizations, "a variety of workshops, seminars, conferences, and retreat

---

57. Marty, *A Nation of Behavers*, 4–6.

58. Ibid., 52–203.

59. Ibid., 204.

60. Martin E. Marty, "Where the Energies Go," *The Annals of the American Academy of Political and Social Science* 527 (May 1993) 11.

61. Ibid., 15.

62. Wade Clark Roof, *Spiritual Marketplace: Baby Boomers and the Remaking of American Religion* (Princeton: Princeton University Press, 1999) 9–10.

centers."[63] This spiritual marketplace produces newsletters, meditation cassettes, self-help groups, books, magazines, and music.[64]

This shift to the "personal, private, and autonomous" in an ever-expanding "spiritual marketplace" has its roots, at least in the United States, in developments that became particularly prominent in the second half of the twentieth century. According to Roof, during this time period "the images and symbols of religion have undergone a quiet transformation."[65] Although Herberg's mid-twentieth century classic *Protestant, Catholic, Jew* provided a quite satisfactory summary of the American religious experience when it was published,[66] in recent decades many Americans have begun to create a new language to articulate their faith and beliefs, which are becoming more eclectic at the same time that their commitments are becoming more private.

Robert Wuthnow frames the changes in terms of different experiences of spirituality. He describes a profound change in our spiritual practices that he believes has occurred since 1950 as "a traditional spirituality of inhabiting sacred places has given way to a new spirituality of seeking—that people have been losing faith in a metaphysic that can make them feel at home in the universe and that they increasingly negotiate among completing glimpses of the sacred, seeking partial knowledge and practical wisdom."[67]

63. Liesa Stamm, "The Influence of Religion and Spirituality in Shaping American Higher Education," in Arthur W. Chickering, Jon C. Dalton, and Liesa Stamm, *Encouraging Authenticity and Spirituality in Higher Education* (San Francisco: Jossey-Bass, 2006), 71.

64. Ibid.

65. Roof, *Spiritual Marketplace*, 3.

66. In commenting on a recent report, "Beyond the God Gap: A New Roadmap for Reaching Religious Americans on Public Policy Issues," discussing how Catholics and Protestants today are reaching and being reached on public policy issues, Martin Marty observed: "What is clear from this and countless other opinion surveys is that the old standard typified by Will Herberg's 1955 classic, *Protestant, Catholic, and Jew*, would be almost useless in changed America. What Herberg called 'Protestant' stood for 'White Mainline Protestants' (WMPs). He hardly noticed what today are termed 'White Evangelical Protestants' (WEPs) or 'African American Protestants' (AAPs). These are the two groups where the 'reaching from and to' is most strenuous, effective, and controversial today." Martin E. Marty, "Reporting on the God Gap," *Sightings*, July 12, 2010. Online: http://divinity.uchicago.edu/martycenter/publications/sightings/archive_2010/0712.shtml.

67. Robert Wuthnow, *After Heaven: Spirituality in America since the 1950s* (Berkeley: University of California Press, 1998) 3.

The traditional "spirituality of dwelling" emphasizes *habitation*. It views God as occupying "a definite place in the universe and creates a sacred space in which humans too can dwell; to inhabit sacred space is to know its territory and to feel secure." A "spirituality of seeking," by contrast, "emphasized *negotiation:* individuals search for sacred moments that reinforce their conviction that the divine exists, but these moments are fleeting; rather than knowing the territory, people explore new special vistas, and they may have to negotiate among complex and confusing meanings of spirituality."[68] Rather than abandoning "religion," Wuthnow suggests that many Americans are, in their spiritual quest, reordering how they relate to "the sacred." At the end of the twentieth century, "growing numbers of Americans piece together their faith like a patchwork quilt. Spirituality has become a vastly complex quest in which each person seeks in his or her own way."[69]

Both forms of spirituality—"dwelling" and "seeking"—have historical precedents in Western religions. Dwelling spirituality draws upon stories of the Garden of Eden and of the Promised Land. Its history has focused on temple religion, and it is expressed prominently during the time of the ascendancy of priests and kings. Seeking spirituality, in contrast, draws upon stories about the tabernacle. It is the faith of pilgrims and sojourners. It is prominent in the Diaspora, as it emphasizes prophets and judges, rather than priests and kings.[70]

In the United States, this shift from "dwelling" to "seeking" accompanied the dramatic social changes that occurred beginning in the late 1950s, increasing in the 1960s, and continuing into the 1970s. As they experienced these social changes, Americans altered their way of perceiving religion and spirituality as they began to revise the beliefs and practices that had come to them in tradition, which included the meaning of the sacred itself. In the early decades of the twentieth century, "a spirituality of dwelling" which emphasized "habitation" was dominant. In this view, religious people sought "social belonging" through involvement in churches and synagogues. As they inhabited these "sacred spaces," they felt connected to known territory, which made them secure. As they began to shift to a "spirituality of seeking," they focused more on developing personal meaning, searching for moments that could

68. Ibid., 3–4.
69. Ibid., 2.
70. Ibid., 4.

reassure them that the divine exists, even if those moments were fleeting. They explored new vistas of spirituality rather than remaining in the comfort of known territories, and they developed personal meaning as they negotiated among different meanings of spirituality.[71]

Spiritual seekers, less concerned with group identity or social location than with a quest for an authentic inner life, focused on questions such as "Does religion relate to my life?" "How can I find spiritual meaning and depth?," and "What might faith mean to me?"[72] Concerned more with "personal meaning" than with "social belonging," many Americans now go beyond the religious institutions with which they have been connected to seek answers. "Growing numbers of people shop for spirituality at New Age and recovery bookstores or pick up spiritual tips from films, talk shows, and news specials on television . . . Many people take classes that expose them to science, secular philosophy, and the teaching of world religions."[73]

As individuals increasingly take more responsibility for shaping their own meaning systems, religious institutions, too, are adapting to these changes, designing services to meet the needs of a population seeking personal spiritual fulfillment. But even as religious institutions seek to adapt to these changing expectations, "large numbers of Americans participate in a variety of workshops and self-help groups, struggle with addictions, undergo therapy, become involved in retreat centers, and are exposed to endless diverse offerings about spirituality in the media."[74] Consequently, spiritual seekers frequently piece together their own belief systems from a range of sources as they create their own practice of religion and spirituality. Thus, as Marty suggested happens over time, a new mapping of the religious scene is required: "New maps are called for when old ways of describing religion fail to capture what is happening in our everyday lives. . . . Boundaries separating one faith tradition from another that once seemed fixed are now blurred; religious identifies are malleable and multifaceted, often overlapping several traditions."[75]

This new map will certainly need to be attentive to the many ways in which people in our culture are seeking to clarify their own sense of

71. Ibid., 3–14.

72. Roof, *Spiritual Marketplace*, 7.

73. Wuthnow, *After Heaven*, 2.

74. Ibid.

75. Roof, *Spiritual Marketplace*, 4.

spirituality, a term that usually has reference to religion in the sense of tradition, but for others is not bound by doctrinal, creedal, or ecclesiastical categories. A broadly based group of leaders came to the following conclusion about what an adequate definition of the term spirituality would have to include:

> Spirituality is a very difficult word to define. An adequate definition would include reference to a relationship with something beyond myself (known as "Creator," "God," "transcendent power," etc.) that is intangible but also real. It would recognize that spirituality is the source of one's values and meaning, a way of understanding the world, an awareness of my "inner self," and a means of integrating the various aspects of myself into a whole.[76]

DEFINING SPIRITUALITY

Thus far we have been discussing spirituality and religiosity, or spiritual and religious, as if they are closely linked or even interchangeable.[77] Current conceptions of spirituality, however, especially among college youth, often do not view them this way, or even as related.[78] While for many, spirituality continues to be closely linked with religion, a growing number of individuals identify their spirituality as either loosely, or not at all, associated with an established religious tradition. This distinction may be enhanced by the college experience. One male student commented, for example:

> I think [the distinction between spirituality and religiosity] is something unique to actually being at college. I never heard anyone distinguish between spirituality and religion when I was back home at my high school and junior high. They were always the same thing. Then I got to college, where you are allowed to be more free-thinking or whatever . . . That's when I started to see that there could be a difference between the two.[79]

76. Steve Jacobsen, *Heart to God, Hands to Work: Connecting Spirituality and Work* (Bethesda, MD: Alban Institute, 1997) 11, quoted in Roof, *Spiritual Marketplace*, 35.

77. Cf. Alyssa N. Bryant and Helen S. Astin, "The Correlates of Spiritual Struggle during the College Years," *Journal of Higher Education* 79.1 (Jan/Feb 2008) 1–27 and note 1.

78. Robert D. Putnam and David E. Campbell, *American Grace: How Religion Divides and Unites Us* (New York: Simon & Schuster, 2010) 120–32.

79. Jennifer A. Lindholm, "The 'Interior' Lives of American College Students: Preliminary Findings from a National Study," in *Passing on the Faith: Transforming*

In light of this, some scholars—especially social scientists—are increasingly suggesting that it is important to clarify how "religion" and "spirituality" may have some similarities but can be distinguished from each other. Wayne Teasdale, for example, suggests:

> Being *religious* connotes belonging to and practicing a religious tradition. Being spiritual suggests a personal commitment to a process of inner development that engages us in our totality. Religion, of course, is one way many people are spiritual. Often, when authentic faith embodies an individual's spirituality the religious and the spiritual will coincide. Still, not every religious person is spiritual (although they ought to be) and not every spiritual person is religious. *Spirituality* is a way of life that affects and includes every moment of existence. It is at once a contemplative attitude, a disposition to a life of depth, and the search for ultimate meaning, direction, and belonging. The spiritual person is committed to growth as an essential ongoing life goal. To be spiritual requires us to stand on our own two feet while being nurtured and supported by our tradition, if we are fortunate enough to have one.[80]

Teasdale's description of spirituality is very general and it coincides with the description provided by theologian James Nelson, who states simply: "In the most general sense, by spirituality I mean the ways and patterns by which the person—intellectually, emotionally, and physically—relates to that which is ultimately real and worthwhile for him or her."[81] Teasdale, unlike Nelson, seems to denigrate those who rely too much on institutions, which he suggests press them to conform to "external piety," and prefers that those involved in the spiritual quest do it on their own through "inner direction." He writes: "A genuinely spiritual person passionately commits to this spiritual development. He or she knows that life is a spiritual journey, and that each one of us must take this journey alone, even while surrounded by loved ones."[82]

Traditions for the Next Generation of Jews, Christians, and Muslims, ed. James L. Heft (New York: Fordham University Press, 2006) 86.

80. Wayne Teasdale, *The Mystic Heart* (Novato, CA: New World Library, 1999) 17–18.

81. James B. Nelson, *The Intimate Connection: Male Sexuality, Masculine Spirituality* (Philadelphia: Westminster, 1988) 21.

82. Teasdale, *The Mystic Heart*, 18.

Spirituality so conceived may, but does not necessarily, make reference to "the sacred."

The development of spirituality is seldom totally separated from other dimensions of personal development, however. Sharon Daloz Parks, for example, connects spirituality to faith and "meaning making" as she writes:

> We human beings seem unable to survive, and certainly cannot thrive, unless we make meaning. We need to be able to make some sort of sense out of things; we seek pattern, order, coherence, and relation in the disparate elements of our experience. If life is perceived as only fragmented and chaotic, we suffer confusion, distress, stagnation, and finally despair.
>
> This capacity and demand for meaning is what I invite the reader to associate with the word *faith.* . . . Faith is often linked exclusively to belief, particularly to religious belief. But faith goes beyond religious belief, parochially understood. Faith is more adequately recognized as *the activity of seeking and discovering meaning in the most comprehensive dimensions of our experience.* Faith is a broad, generic human experience. To be human is to dwell in faith, to dwell in the sense one makes out of life—what seems ultimately true and dependable about self, world, and cosmos (whether that meaning be strong or fragile, expressed in religious or secular terms). This way of understanding the nature of faith has value for secular and religious folk alike. It addresses our culture's current hunger for a shared language about things "spiritual."[83]

Relating this specifically to the experience of men, the authors of a recent exploration of the identity and spirituality of younger men—one of the few studies of which we are aware that focuses specifically on the spirituality of young men as men—describe spirituality in a way that relates it broadly to many aspects of human experience.

> Spirituality represents the deepest level of the human quest for meaning and hope. Spirituality is associated with identity—who am I, and how I fit in the universe. Although not everyone would claim to be religious or even claim to believe in God, they are spiritual, they have a deeper sense of self and making meaning in the world. A person's spirituality provides a frame of reference

---

83. Sharon Daloz Parks, *Big Questions, Worthy Dreams: Mentoring Young Adults in Their Search for Meaning, Purpose, and Faith* (San Francisco: Jossey-Bass, 2000) 7.

for the whole of life utilizing language, beliefs, values, personal morality, and public ethics.[84]

This is, for now, the best working definition we have for "spirituality," and one of its greatest strengths is that it links various dimensions of one's life together, including aspects of one's inner life, meaning making, personal morality, and public ethics. The reference to "meaning making" fits well with Parks's delineation of faith, construed as "to dwell in the sense one makes out of life—what seems ultimately true and dependable about self, world and cosmos (whether that meaning be strong or fragile, expressed in religious or secular terms)." This does not require that a person of faith makes reference to a "transcendent" reality or an "ultimate" power, often referred to as "the sacred," but it is very compatible with it. Indeed, many scholars of religion believe that to be human is to be *homo religiosus*. The popular religious writer, Karen Armstrong, believes that all religion fills essentially the same function: it offers meaning in its reach for transcendence. "Religion was not something tacked on to the human condition," Armstrong writes in *A Case for God*. "The desire to cultivate a sense of the transcendent may be the defining human characteristic."[85]

We will discuss this further in our chapter that analyzes the self-identification of the college men we interviewed, including those who might say "I am spiritual but not religious."

SPIRITUALITY IN HIGHER EDUCATION

We haven't found a lot of empirical research focusing specifically on college-age men's spirituality, but from our experience on different campuses in different parts of the country, we sense that the standards of masculinity in our country, which we have discussed earlier, make it difficult for college men to acknowledge their spiritual natures, especially to other men. Yet, research suggests that spirituality is vitally important to the great majority of college students—men as well as women.[86] Compounding the situation is the fact that most colleges and

84. David W. Anderson, Paul G. Hill, and Roland D. Martinson, *Coming of Age: Exploring the Identity and Spirituality of Younger Men* (Minneapolis: Augsburg Fortress, 2006) 160.

85. Quoted by Amy Frykholm, "Tracking God," *Christian Century* (June 29, 2010) 21.

86. Alexander W. Astin and Helen S. Astin, *The Spiritual Life of College Students: A National Study of College Students' Search for Meaning and Purpose.* Higher Education

universities, especially public institutions, do little to acknowledge and nurture the "inner" development of young people—the sphere of values and beliefs, emotional maturity, moral development, spirituality, and self-understanding.[87] The academic programs of most institutions of higher education rarely acknowledge that human beings have a spiritual dimension, much less endeavor to develop it. To think, for example, "of the professor as a guide may make any number of teachers and administrators uneasy. It is a problematic concept [especially] for public institutions in a culture committed to 'separation of church and state.'"[88]

The areas where spirituality is addressed—namely, chaplaincies and programs run by local churches or other religious communities—tend to be marginal, sectarian, and too traditionally religious for many students. Thus, when men enter institutions of higher learning in the United States, laboring under the strain of the standards of conventional masculinity, they find an entire aspect of their lives unrecognized, with few opportunities for development. Both the neglect of spirituality and the uncritical acceptance of dominant masculine ideals do much to distort men as whole human beings and bring much unhappiness to their present and future lives.

Aware of this paucity of attention given to the development of spirituality in students in colleges and universities, the Higher Education Research Institute, housed in the Graduate School of Education at UCLA, launched a seven-year research project, "Spirituality in Higher Education: Students' Search for Meaning and Purpose," in 2003, supported by the Templeton Foundation. It examined changes in students' spiritual development and religious qualities during their college years,

Research Institute (HERI), 2003, online: http://www.spirituality.ucla.edu/docs/reports/Spiritual_Life_College_Students_Full_Report.pdf; Jeffrey R. Young, "Survey Finds Spiritual Leanings Among Most College Students," *Chronicle of Higher Education* (Nov. 28, 2003) A36; Vachel W. Miller and Merle M. Ryan, *Transforming Campus Life: Reflections on Spirituality and Religious Pluralism,* Studies in Education and Spirituality (New York: Peter Lang, 2001); Chickering, Dalton, and Stamm, *Coming of Age*; Michael K. Herndon, "Expressions of Spirituality among African-American College Males," *Journal of Men's Studies* 12.1 (Fall 2003) 75–84; John Bennett, "Spirituality and the Vitality of Academic Life," *Journal of College and Character* 4.9 (2003), online: http://journals.naspa.org/jcc/vol4/iss9/2/; Alyssa N. Bryant, "Assessing Contexts and Practices for Engaging Students' Spirituality," *Journal of College and Character* 10.2 (2008), online: http://journals.naspa.org/jcc/vol10/iss2/10/; Parks, *Big Questions, Worthy Dreams.*

87. Lindholm, "The 'Interior' Lives of American College Students," 97–100.

88. Parks, *Big Questions, Worthy Dreams,* 166.

seeking to determine what role the colleges played in facilitating those developments.[89]

Directed by Alexander Astin, Helen Astin, and Jennifer Lindholm, the project was designed to enhance our understanding of how college students perceive spirituality and the role that spirituality plays in their lives. The researchers conducted interviews with individual students, held focus groups, and interviewed faculty. They collected and analyzed data from 14,527 students at 136 colleges and universities. In their findings, they distinguished "five spiritual qualities" from "five religious qualities." The religious qualities they identified were religious commitment, religious engagement, religious/social conservatism, religious skepticism, and religious struggle, but what they were primarily interested in were the spiritual qualities: spiritual quest, equanimity, ethic of caring, charitable involvement, and ecumenical worldview.[90] In fact, they defined spirituality as a "multifaceted quality" that involves "an active quest for life's big questions (Spiritual Quest), a global worldview that transcends ethnocentricism (Ecumenical Worldview), a sense of caring and compassion for others (Ethic of Caring) coupled with a lifestyle that includes service of others (Charitable Involvement), and a capacity to maintain one's sense of calm and centeredness, especially in times of stress (Equanimity)."[91] They concluded that students' religious engagement declines somewhat during college, whereas their spiritual development, which encouraged students toward greater expansiveness, grows substantially.[92]

Some observers have noted that the UCLA study emphasizes "spirituality" without paying much attention to its religious roots. They have expressed concern that spirituality that is not rooted in religious tradition can quickly lapse into narcissism. "The pursuit of meaning and the exercise of life commitments are enriched when they are informed by tradition, religious practices that have evolved through the centuries,

89. Alexander W. Astin, Helen S. Astin, and Jennifer A. Lindholm, *Cultivating the Spirit: How College Can Enhance Students' Inner Lives* (San Francisco: Jossey-Bass, 2011).

90. Ibid., 18–19.

91. "Spirituality in Higher Education: A National Study of College Students' Search for Meaning and Purpose," Overall Findings. Online: http://www.spirituality.ucla.edu/findings/.

92. Astin, Astin, and Lindholm, *Cultivating the Spirit*, 89–92, 115–36.

and an informed understanding of the role of religious faith in shaping our collective identity."[93]

While we are not totally satisfied with how spirituality and religion are distinguished in this book by Astin, Astin, and Lindholm, our own concern is to focus more specifically on how college men experience and develop their spirituality in relation to their masculinity. While paying less attention to what can be done in the classroom, we are convinced that developing spirituality and addressing the burdensome masculine standards are goals that can be effectively met through innovative programs in the co-curricula of student life that bring men together in small groups to reflect on their lives. The exploration and development of spirituality in men's groups can provide an implicit challenge to conventional masculine norms and a crucible for envisioning ways of being male. At the same time, the critical scrutiny of traditional masculinity frees men to enhance their spiritual dimension by challenging the beliefs that would have them regard spirituality as unworthy of "real" men. We will explore how this has been done by examining the interviews with college men we conducted on seven campuses that pursued the development of men's groups in many different formats.

93. Don Miller and Jim Heft, quoted by James L. Heft, "Introduction: Youth and Continuity of Religion Traditions," in *Passing on the Faith*, ed. James L. Heft (New York: Fordham University Press, 2006) 2.

4

Masculinity, Spirituality, and the Measures of Being a Man

THIS CHAPTER ANALYZES THE findings from audiotaped interviews with thirty-six students who were recruited as part of this project. Each student was enrolled at one of seven private liberal arts colleges: Augustana College in Illinois, Gustavus Adolphus College in Minnesota, Luther College in Iowa, Saint John's University in Minnesota, Siena College in New York, the University of Portland in Oregon, and Wagner College in New York.

The seven small, four-year colleges at which we conducted the interviews had 2011–2012 total costs in the range of $40,000 to $50,000 per annum (tuition, fees, room and board, books, transportation, and personal items). All thirty-six interviewees thus came from backgrounds of some financial privilege, or were high enough achievers to have been granted significant scholarships.

Interviews were conducted by members of the research team, and each interview lasted approximately ninety minutes. This produced at least fifty-six hours of taped data to analyze. In particular, data pertaining to issues of masculinity, emotions, and spirituality are analyzed and compared in this chapter. All names given for students who are quoted in this chapter are pseudonyms and the particular colleges in which they studied will not be indicated in order to allow the speakers to remain unidentifiable due to the nature of some of their comments about the schools in which they were studying.

In those fifty-six hours of taped interviews, many models of masculinity over the recent decade are presented and, of course, there is no one model that appealed to all of the interviewees, in spite of their having the group experiences in common. Different schools attract different students. Different men's spirituality groups had different leaders and different internal agendas, and most of the students were at an age where expressing a personal opinion was a very important part of establishing a unique identity. As well, the academic institutions at which these men studied had a great deal in common, but this should not be allowed to mask the differences of opinion and definition.

"I AM THE CONSULATE FOR MASCULINITY" (MAX)

At one point in the interview process, Miles repeated a question from the interviewers and then answered sagely: "How do I do masculinity? I guess I try to embrace the things I'm passionate about that aren't necessarily considered masculine by a lot of people."

Miles was responding to a stock question that was used in all the interviews, asking the young men to identify one particular activity or involvement that summarized the way each of the men understood what was unique about the way he lived out his masculinity. The question they were asked can be summarized as "I am masculine when I—." The range of answers illustrates the breadth of understandings of masculinity lived out by the men. A significant minority of the men concentrated on playing sports—including "beating my girlfriend at basketball" (Steve)—or outdoor activities, such as hunting, fishing, or driving a pickup truck. Others were even flippant in their answers, perhaps suggesting that the question was worded in a way that they didn't take seriously: "My handwriting is very masculine" (Mason) or "Smoking a cigar" (Jason).

But other answers revealed how broadly "doing masculinity" was being redefined, approaching the subject in some cases with personal qualities such as exercising one's gifts as a leader (Darrell, Steve, and Jarad), being compassionate, modeling self-confidence or relational honesty, or having an open door for those in need. Yet others chose to focus on specific acts of charity that defined their masculinity: taking care of my aging family members (Tom), sacrificing my own needs for those of others (Vince, Nelson), teaching other men how to talk about their emotions or how to take a stand on something (Simon, Marc), or the importance of finding and affirming the best of one's personal qualities. Some men were also quick to identify specific actions or activities that they felt to be quite antithetical to healthy masculinity. Two such unhealthy things were pointed to by more than one research participant in each case. The first was "using sex with women to advance your own social standing or as proof that you're really cool." The second was articulated well by both Max and Taylor: "You will never learn to be manly by sitting in front of a computer screen in your room all day playing video games."

FATHERS AND OTHER ROLE MODELS

About one third of the research participants made reference to the role of their fathers or grandfathers in shaping their masculinity. Historically and customarily, young men learned "the ways of men" from their fathers and grandfathers, and this was the case with a number of the young men we interviewed. The value of personal example was affirmed by Mason: "Having a great father helps younger men understand masculinity better."

Colin, Jerome, and Jace each praised their fathers for shaping their masculinity and each added an extra twist to the praise. Colin said, "My father taught me how to be a man authentically, and how important it is to keep spirituality separate from religion," a distinction that showed up in other places in this research. Jerome praised his father's ability to reveal several differing sides of himself regularly: "My dad is not taken in by the idea that you have to look more attractive; he's definitely the farthest from that. He enjoys himself, he goes gardening, he cries at movies, he—I mean, he is, you know, he's masculine but he is very feminine too and he's totally okay with that." So obviously was Jerome. Jace pointed out how both his parents had taught him about gender roles: "Most of my masculinity comes from my dad—just from behaving like him and emulating him. My dad can be really masculine, and my mom can be really feminine. But I guess maybe because of that, I've kind of integrated both of them a little bit more." Miles also understood the importance of learning from both parents, after having been asked at a program-sponsored retreat what he learned about masculinity from his father, and what he learned about masculinity from his mother.

But a significant minority of the men who chose to speak about their fathers did so with regret about the ways in which their fathers' masculinities did not encourage the sons to adopt a healthy gender role.

For example, Jeremy said, "I try to emulate the type of masculinity that my parents value, but I'm not interested in it, really." Mason's disappointment was echoed by several others: "I'm sorry my father, a good man, was unable to talk about feelings or relationships." Mason and his peers were giving voice to the pain and sorrow that young men carry when their fathers have been too distant. Guy Corneau wrote about this in his now-classic book, *Absent Fathers, Lost Sons*.[1] Fathers who don't know how to father their children frequently have not been well-fathered themselves. Unfortunately, this lack of paternal affirmation and support often leaves sons lost, empty, and even disoriented. As Jarad remarked, "My father didn't help me learn how to be a man. A group can help me, but in the end, I've had to go it alone." Sons internalize their fathers, just as they internalize their mothers. Jace remarked on this: "I've got a father. I have that idea of masculinity within myself." Sons internalize their failed fathers just as deeply as they internalize their affirming fathers.

"MASCULINITY IS THE PRACTICE OF EVERYDAY LIFE" (ABE)

Most of us who work now in the field of Men's Studies in Religion understand that masculinity is a social construction, a socially dictated set of roles, rules, and expectations that are generated not only from within an individual or by a family system, but more often by a culture and society at large. Of course, there are many supportive actors in a socially generated script, and so we attribute constructions to cultures, societies, religions, families, individuals, external environments, educational institutions, and life experiences, all acted out, in public and in private, on the stage that Michel de Certeau called "the practice of everyday life."[2] Indeed, Abe seemed to have been reading Certeau, for he said, "I think that spirituality is like masculinity . . . It's what one individual believes, and how they choose to practice that in everyday life."

The vast majority of the research participants rejected any suggestion that there is a one-size-fits-all masculinity. In a variety of settings and through their own life experiences, they had discovered for themselves that many different masculinities can be performed, though some are more widely sanctioned than others. Adam explained, however,

---

1. Guy Corneau, *Absent Fathers, Lost Sons: The Search for Masculine Identity* (Boston: Shambhala, 1991).

2. Michel de Certeau, *The Practice of Everyday Life*, trans. Steven Rendall (Berkeley: University of California Press, 1984).

that even wanting to talk about masculinities can sometimes generate a negative reaction.

> I doubt that we would get every guy to participate [in a men's group]. I just think there are some guys that are just, you know, "Why would I talk about masculinity? Why do I have to, like, you know, I'm a guy; I like girls, I like—you know." We try not to set barriers on what masculinity is because we're just trying to explore, you know, what it is today? The thing is that a lot of guys are just like, "No, I know I'm a guy, you know—here [pointing to their heads] and down there [pointing to their pants]."

All of our research participants were quite clear that there are groups of men on college campuses who are not interested in exploring what either masculinity or spirituality means, for their own individual reasons.

Aaron gave a rather full definition of masculinity as a particular type of performance, and then brought his own critique to that definition:

> There are a lot of ways to be masculine. I mean, there's the usual socially constructed way that would be like, you know, being strong, being tough, a lot of times being almost emotionless. But I guess that's not the way that I see a true man being. I think a true man, like a person who is masculine, kind of owns up to the full range of his emotions and understands his emotions and doesn't just swallow them. So I guess I see masculinity as knowing yourself and that way I think you're a true man if you know who you are and where you come from and you can own up to that. Masculinity has to do with personal authenticity and is not dictated by other men.

He went on to expand his observation that there are many ways to be masculine by adding, "Masculinity has to do with personal authenticity, and is not dictated by other men." Most of our interviewees took a similar approach to masculinity. Max, for example, observed how difficult masculinity is to define. He pointed out that different fields of inquiry define it differently—for example, biologically speaking, it's simply someone with an X chromosome and a Y chromosome. He continued, "But I also believe that gender roles are very much attributed to society's rules. For example, my family is nontraditional in the sense that my father was the stay-at-home parent my entire life and my mother worked." Certainly, it would seem that Jason was correct in observing that "No one explains what it means to be a man. It just comes at you passively from many directions."

Many of the participants had spent hours in their groups, and a lot of personal time, thinking about what it means to be masculine. Max continued:

> The stereotypical role of masculinity is that men need to be in control, and men need to be physically strong and capable of ruling, and be very decisive and very sure of themselves, but not have any emotion, and they essentially need to be like very stoic sorts of rulers. And my perspective on masculinity is that that's not the case at all.

Vince appeared to define masculinity at an even more personal level. "I try not to think about whether I'm masculine or not because it boxes me in. I don't want to do anything just because someone thinks it's a manly thing to do. What's important is how you feel about yourself at the end of the day." Very few of the interviewees named specific models of "good" masculinity other than an occasional male parent or male teacher. Morris said, "I reject any notion that masculinity has certain mandatory standards of behavior. Men can choose to break as many molds as they wish." Taylor summed up an attitude common among almost all our interviewees: "I don't agree with definitions of masculinity that include being confident, athletic, strong, tough, and very lumberjack." It wasn't that our interviewees felt these roles were wrong per se, but that too many men got trapped in one or two of those roles, unable to express the full range of roles and emotions that should characterize the many ways in which masculinity is performed and that are constantly evolving.

A few of the research participants weren't willing to push definitions that far. For instance, Nate commented, "Different people have different definitions of masculinity, but most of them still include not talking about our feelings." Jeff added: "Masculinity is measured by the quality of the relationships it generates." Once one has decided to perform a certain type of masculinity, or set of masculinities, "look around you for models for the masculinity you can emulate," suggested Brice. This is possible, according to Adam, because "masculinity is not becoming more definite, it's becoming more infinite." There is already more than one socially sanctioned form of masculinity, according to Dillon: the "social masculinity, which we've learned to deconstruct in our group, and then there's personal masculinity, where you take your own stance within social masculinity." At this point in the history of the evolution of genders, "each man has his own version of masculinity, and there's no need to imitate others" (Keagan).

IS IT POSSIBLE TO DISTINGUISH TRUE MASCULINITY FROM FALSE MASCULINITY?

Some, though not all, of our interviewees spoke about whether a definition of "true masculinity," as opposed to the various "false masculinities," could be found. Adam was among those who struggled with the impossibility of defining "true masculinity." He said,

> I have a certain set of definitions of what being a good person is and so if I can lead by example and help others to be an overall good person, then I think I've done my job of being a good male. Representing true masculinity is being, maybe, a male figure that other males can live up to and they aspire to and, you know, if I'm leaving this planet a better place and I inspire others to do so, then I think I've carried out my job of, you know, defining masculinity.

But in the same interview, he also admitted that "there is no single masculinity, no 'true' masculinity. Masculinity is shaped by one's life course, one's experiences, and one's goals in life."

Students on campus looked around themselves and saw a variety of masculinities being played out, or performed. They spoke of wanting to invite other young men to break out of those stereotypical masculinities and find other ways to express their gender identity. Colin observed, "In the group of false masculinity, you have this macho group of guys that are just doing stuff for themselves and don't care about anybody else." He felt that the promotion of an "authentic" masculinity, a healthier masculinity, would come infectiously as young men on campuses comfortably lived out masculinities other than the macho one—which as Abe pointed out, consists mostly of "girls and football and beer." Having defined a false masculinity, Colin went on to define "true" masculinity: "A real man breaks norms; stands up for truth, justice, and the right things; and is unafraid of being introspective. Masculinity is something that's deeper than religion, even deeper at the core of men. It's something that I feel has been stifled a lot in our culture. Being a real man with authentic masculinity is about defying that, breaking the norm, standing up for truth and justice and what is right, and being open to that introspection and not forcing one's views on other people."

In other words, to Colin, true masculinity is both intentionally exemplary and tolerant of any difference that exhibits authenticity. Abe expressed the same thought in different words—"Masculinity is about being comfortable with your choices and not performing stereotypes"— as did Aaron: "You're a true man if you know who you are and where you come from, and you can own up to that. A true man, like a person who is masculine, owns up to his emotions and understands his emotions and doesn't just swallow them." Several other interviewees also used the expression "being true to myself" when defining masculinity. Vince expanded on that: "The true people that I see don't care what others think, and they can stand out and just be leaders, and if not, they're okay with that. I think that's true masculinity, because you're aware of who you are and you're fine with it."

As researchers with a long history in Men's Studies in Religion, we were caught off guard by one image that was used by three different interviewees, each from a different college. Adam's words exemplify what each of the three said: "I don't want to leave the world in the red. So I make sure it's a better place for the people behind me than it was when I came in, and I think that would be, you know, that true masculinity will be evaluated at the Judgment Day. When I'm faced with my Creator, I'll find out whether I was masculine. It probably won't be the way we define it presently." Masculinity is generally viewed by social scientists and scholars of gender as a set of social performances, constructed and, at times, intentionally adopted or adapted. Masculinity is generally not viewed as a theological category in contemporary discourse, though it was considered a theological category in early church history, when "playing the man" was an active social role available to males and to exceptionally devout females.[3]

CONFRONTING SUPERMAN

Hegemonic masculinity—the overarching social construct that measures and judges each man's efforts to live up to the social construc-

3. See, for example, Peter Brown, *The Body and Society: Men, Women, and Sexual Renunciation in Early Christianity* (New York: Columbia University Press, 1988), and Gillian Cloke, *This Female Man of God: Women and Spiritual Power in the Patristic Age, 350–450 AD* (New York: Routledge, 1995).

tion's hypothesized male identity and behavior—does not like to be challenged.[4] Michael Kimmel has discussed the "marketplace man," a superpowered image of white masculinity designed to perpetuate the inequalities of the corporate world, and has emphasized how punitive it could be.[5] Our young interviewees were quite articulate about the languaging and defensiveness of traditional masculinity that seeks to thwart all redefinitions of what is acceptable and what is not. Like Kimmel, our interviewees also had labels for these various dangerous attempts to entrench a specific kind of masculinity as the only truly "authentic" one. In the interviews, they referred to the following:

The Big Man Ladder—A figurative and symbolic ladder, shown to young boys in the hopes of training them to climb, rung by rung, the ladder to a particular type of adult masculinity. (Keith)

Dude Talk—The way that men structure their conversations with each other to make sure their emotions never become apparent. (Taylor)

The Man Box—"If you go outside the man box, you're going outside all those stereotypes. You're going outside what people expect men to be. You're outside that closed-mindedness—that unwillingness to be an individual, and not just to go along with what every other man wants." (Abe)

The Man Complex—A set of self-confidence issues, from within which young men worry about their looks, whether young women see them as desirable, and whether they are able to measure up to social expectations of someone with a successful future. (Jeremy)

The Man Fortress—"Some guys at a group meeting were telling about why they were there and I just said, 'Yeah, the males of the last few generations have watched the feminist movement, maybe admired it and supported it, but now that we've been left behind, we might as well build a fortress.' It's kind of a glass shield, the armor, the . . . I don't know, the body piercings, the tattoos, whatever you want to do . . . the things seen as armor." (Taylor)

Man Talk—"Group is a very comfortable setting—the fact that they are other men, and then it goes back to the masculinity thing. We talk about things that we know women just won't understand. It could be something completely random, has nothing to do with being a man, but something that women will just not understand, and then we talk about those things." (Jeremy)

The Masculine Front—"There's some stuff in the research about what's called the masculine front, and it's where we are men and have this certain thing that we feel we have to project, that people kind of expect of us or that we want to project but on the inside we actually feel different than that. We may feel really more vulnerable, we may be scared to death, but we're acting like we're tough or we are maybe not completely sure of our self but we will put up that masculine front." (Garett)

The young men in our research were painfully aware of the social expectations that could be laid upon them and how confining these could be, and so, in the window of opportunity provided by the men's spirituality groups, they began to reconstruct these definitions as a first step toward the possibility of finding different ways to define themselves and to perform their masculinity publicly after college.

MASCULINITY AS THE PERFORMANCE OF SET ROLES

In 1990, about the time that many of our interviewees were born, anthropologist David Gilmore published his influential book *Manhood in the Making.*[6] His book made a powerful impact in both Men's Studies and Men's Studies in Religion. Gilmore argued that across human history, males have played three metaroles: Protector, Provider, and Impregnator (though subsequently, some scholars of Men's Studies have reinterpreted this as Procreator in order to decrease the sexual aspect and allow room for poets and musicians, inventors, and theoreticians). While our interviewees did not seem familiar with Gilmore's work, some

6. David Gilmore, *Manhood in the Making: Cultural Concepts of Masculinity* (New Haven: Yale University Press, 1990).

of their responses could be interpreted as reflecting Gilmore's theories that males play particular culturally-determined social roles designed to protect and advance a society.

Interviewees grasped the traditional masculine role of Protector, and gave it their own spin. Blain described his own protector role this way: "I demonstrate masculinity through working with children, trying to steer them onto the right path. I also demonstrate my masculinity by taking care of my younger siblings, protecting my family members." Ted was somewhat more traditional in his understanding: "I think masculinity is in large part being like a protector of a family, not just the breadwinner."

Blain was finding his role as protector within his own family: "My youngest brother is 13, and he's going through some rough times, so [my role is] just kind of being that person that he can come to and talk to. I'm definitely protective of my siblings; I think that being protective and taking care of my family is still, even though it's the stereotype, I think it's still very important. Not that women can't do it too, obviously, but I think that's an important aspect of masculinity." Steve came from a more conservative position, emphasizing the importance of leading and being in charge as parts of protecting. "I don't know if there's necessarily a clear-cut definition that I can label for masculinity, but I would just say being in charge, being in leadership positions. I think it's emasculating when someone else is telling me what to do and I have no say."

These young men were still in school and so finding examples in their interviews of the Provider role was more difficult. Mark offered: "I had kind of a stereotypical image of what masculinity is about, just being like, kind of being manly, if you will—being a provider generally, like keeping things such as working hard and being a respectful person and respecting others kind of thing. And generally a man like this is what I try to do for the most part. But the definition of masculinity also shouldn't limit me. For example, I find that although I play the piano, which is often something that's kind of a feminine thing to do, I don't find that to be the case, I guess."

Mark's definition, then, of being provider included working hard, but also respecting the needs and wishes of others. He then raised the question of how playing a musical instrument fit with images of masculinity, a conundrum that three of the other interviewees who were musicians also commented on. Nate portrayed just being in a group as one means by which he was regularly providing for others: "With just men, I think you can feel like you can be more open because you feel like they've shared some of the same experiences and they think the way you do." He went on to explain that being open with others is a way of providing for their emotional needs and stoking their self-confidence as young men. Vince claimed "being a decision maker" as a way he provided for others. He helped people clarify their own feelings and opinions and thus make smarter choices, based on the inspiration of his best friend, who had an unusually high moral character.

Our interviewees did not address the role of Impregnator as put forth by Gilmore, but, as has been pointed out, several did mention that their musicianship was an integral part of their masculinity, thus touching on the role of Procreator. As Mark commented in passing, "Being a provider is part of being manly, but then, so is playing the piano."

THE TYPES AND ROLES OF MASCULINITY

Daniel divided masculinities into types that young men find disempowering as opposed to those that young men find constructive: "I think of masculinity as, like, this overarching social force or pressure. There's a big cloud of social forces that say, To be a man is this or this. There are also little subtypes, perhaps. So there are those kinds of masculinity and those are the kinds that I in my life and then we as a group would want to deconstruct immediately. More personal masculinities, by which I mean more constructive masculinities, would be 'Okay, we've been kind of tossed off the gender shackles but what do we do now?'"

However, as we analyzed the research results, we discovered that the research participants had identified many forms of masculinity, or more correctly, many masculinities. In simplistic discussions, people tend to think of there being only one masculinity—usually the one more familiar to us based on culture and life experience, and the one that we as young boys were geared to emulate, usually termed "hegemonic masculinity."

Nearly 50 percent of our research participants mentioned the existence, and promise, of the many masculinities that men can choose from and perform. As Miles put it, "There are many alternative masculinities." Interestingly, a number of these men's comments implied the importance of "rugged individuality"—that is, that each man had a right to define his own masculinity, regardless of what others might think.

For example, Morris said, "I reject any notion that masculinity has certain mandatory standards of behavior," while Brice remarked, "Owning your own masculinity means deciding what *you* think is masculine," and Keagan said, "Each man has his own version of masculinity, and there's no need to imitate others." While it is certainly true, as Nelson observed, that "Masculinity is how much of a man you are, I guess. I mean, that definition is different for different people," Beau's remark seemed to rebalance that: "There are also forms of masculinity that can be found in the worst of men."

Taylor's experience was that "[t]here is no substance to the masculinity if there's not a depth with it. It's just a surface masculinity." Garett chose to point to a particular type of masculinity that appeared to be generally unattractive to most of our research participants: "I'm not interested in endorsing the 'alpha male' as a form of masculinity. The alpha male is a Hollywood stereotype—that stereotypical man, you know, that you see on TV, like some guy that comes in who's real strong and he's that alpha male who thinks he knows what he's doing and kind of takes charge, but really that's not—I don't find that to be masculinity. Fortunately, there are lots of other types of masculinity." Bart seemed, instead, to endorse a masculinity that included being "emotional and vulnerable."

A few of our participants were a bit more skeptical, implying that there were certain behaviors or attitudes that didn't fit the healthy masculinity they were describing and promoting. For example, Alan observed that while there were lots of types of masculinity, they didn't all seem to be healthy ones. Nelson was significantly more pessimistic: "Different people have different definitions of masculinity, but most of them still include not talking about feelings." In the end, Aaron suggested, any form of masculinity could be validated only through one's personal authenticity rather than being dictated by others.

In a sense, the portrait of masculinity created by our research participants was more like a colorful pointillist canvas than like a black-and-white photograph. Our participants were well aware of the subjective determination of any definition of masculinity, as well as the erratic and situational nature of its various performances. Not one of our thirty-six participants was willing to settle for a definition of masculinity that was in any way hegemonic or narrowly boundaried.

One thing the vast majority of our participants agreed upon was that masculinity is generally a social construction, rather than an essentialist difference. Dillon expressed this understanding when he said, "Masculinity can become a healthy component of who we create ourselves as, who we choose to understand ourselves as, just as race is a construct that is oppressive and yet can become a healthy part of your identity." Jason didn't like the idea of being told to be masculine, any more than he assumed that women like being told to be feminine. As he said, "I just don't see myself in those terms." The participants understood that hegemonic masculinity is constructed by culture (Jace); environment (Adam); parents (Jeremy); intergenerational family networks (Max); peers, including students (Jeff); and/or social interactions (Keith). Rather than men acting out their gender in the form of a "Hollywood stereotype" (Garett), Adam succinctly summarized the general position of our participants by saying, "The performance of masculinity is unique to each person." The participants in general were not interested in "stereotypical masculinity" (Keith), but rather wanted to trust themselves to define their own gender identity, not have it defined or labeled by others (Jason). They did not feel a need to continue playing sports just to prove their masculinity (Alan, Jerome) and they wanted to define masculinity for themselves (Brice, Abe). Abe summarized his resistance to any external definition of his own masculinity by stating, "If I have to fake masculinity to hang out with other guys, it's not worth it. What's important is how you feel about yourself at the end of the day."

What, then, did constitute masculinity? For Colin, it was an attitude about life, including the way one interacts with others from the heart—respecting women, other men, and life. For Tom, it was about accepting responsibility for the things we are in charge of but offering the same option to others. For some, masculinity meant being brave enough to leave all behavioral options open (Keith). Jeff said, "I feel masculine when I'm being competitive, but I also feel—my own vision of masculinity when I'm most vulnerable during conversations. Masculinity is measured by the quality of the relationships it generates." For Adam, masculinity meant focusing on one's finest values and then letting those values determine one's behavior. In this same sense, he continued:

> I think a lot of things that are required for good masculinity are required for good femininity: being strong, being confident in yourself, and setting good examples. So if that's how close it is,

then sure, I would consider that I probably have some feminine qualities. There are a lot of things—a lot of internal feelings or internal motivations—that drive great women to be great women, and the characteristics that you see in great women, or women that people label as great, are going to be the same characteristics that you see in great men. So when you get to the core of it, is there a difference between femininity and masculinity? Aside from some physical features and chromosomes, maybe there's not so much a difference. Maybe it's more just an "-inity," and it's just the difference in the beginning of the word.

Keith noted something similar: "I have a harder time drawing that line between masculinity and femininity, because I view things much more from a point of view of equality." For participant Jason, these differences and similarities represented the Godhead: ". . . the way your body is masculine, feminine, if you're a different skin color, whatever, the way your body is—I guess I see that as an expression of the divine."

Not all of our participants identified masculinity as a social construction; about 10 percent took an essentialist position. For example, Beau argued that "men and women are different and were created that way." But whatever the position they took, the participants seemed to agree that hegemonic masculinity was potentially both dangerous and undesirable. Garett observed, "Machismo is a form of ignorance about the negative effects of masculinity." Abe argued that he would rather "'go outside the manbox, resisting the stereotypes, the closed-mindedness, and the conformity." Darrell seemed to agree, arguing that "society's view of masculinity includes a lot of good things, but it's not always correct. For example, you don't need always to be in control."

EMOTIONS AND MASCULINITY

Traditional masculinity has often been defined as characteristically anti-emotional, nonemotional, or emotionally stunted. Perhaps this is why it was so important to the research participants that they become emotionally literate, including being vulnerable. Alan argued that "Masculinity must include emotions, for emotions are a part of masculinity." Aaron characterized his emotions as "one of my manly qualities." Bart felt that "I'm most masculine when I'm relaxed and in touch with my feelings and emotions." Simon also wanted to find his own place within masculinity: "I'm really not the most masculine person in the world . . . But I would call myself masculine in my own right. I'm very comfortable with my body." But not all men know how to do this, and one of the intended outcomes of the spirituality groups was to encourage men to identify, manage, and express their emotions appropriately. That journey was not an easy one for all the participants; as Jarad admitted, "I had no model for what male vulnerability might mean, and so I don't often know how to interpret my own feelings." Nate agreed that while he had been taught at home to express his feelings, many men can't or won't express feelings, assuming alexithymia, or the inability to identify and express emotion in a healthy and relationally constructive manner, to be one of the primary qualities of a manly man. Yet, some of the participants argued that men learn emotional literacy much more easily from other men than from women, and hence emotional literacy featured in the men's spirituality groups.

Vulnerability and emotions are often connected in men's minds, but the research participants understood the importance of men being openly vulnerable. Jeff sometimes felt that vulnerability destroyed the sense of competitiveness he attached to his masculinity; in particular he was worried about being vulnerable "during conversations, especially those about what I'm going through." Yet Taylor remarked, "A real man isn't afraid to do things he's afraid of," and Vince observed, "I feel a disconnect when I'm in an environment where masculinity is defined as meaning not talking about vulnerabilities and emotions, and 'quit being a pansy.'" Bart argued that strength can actually be found in being vulnerable, and that men don't need to put on a show.

In general, many of the research participants were at the beginning of a life-long journey of learning how to find, identify, and express their emotions in ways that left them constructively vulnerable and proud of who they were. But they also resented the messages that tried to shut them back down into a constricted masculinity. As Jerome remarked, "The male emotions that get focused on are anger, dominance, force . . . but men do exhibit kindness and gentleness, you know."

The Supportive Group Experience

A number of the research participants found the opportunity for support and growth in the men's spirituality groups, even when the larger college environment did not feel particularly supportive. Colin observed, "Only some college-age men care about understanding their masculinity in a healthy way," while Alan opined, "Colleges don't understand the atmosphere that young men need in order to be healthy. They're stuck in the past in an older version of masculinity." This did not, however, affect their obvious appreciation for what they gained by participating in the small groups. As Colin observed, "Participating in an all-male group teaches new skills on how to interact with other men, with women, and with society in general." Not only was the group experience a major factor in the young men's exploration of their masculinity and spirituality, but so was the classroom. Keith said, "College courses have helped me keep my masculinity in perspective instead of using it abusively." Adam added, "Teachers model varieties of masculinity for us, which helps guys in our group do masculinity differently."

We will examine other aspects of the dynamics of the men's spirituality groups later in this chapter.

THE DEFINITION AND PRACTICE
OF MASCULINE SPIRITUALITY

Just as the definitions of masculinity explored earlier in this chapter have been shown to be complex, so with the definitions and understandings of spirituality. Within the nature of a small religiously-oriented college is a visibility that shaped the way students thought about the practices of their various spiritualities. For example, their comments often revealed how little of their personal life was invisible. Spirituality, however, often needs to be visible to be feel effective, yet even this expectation is complex. As Miguel noted, "The more you express yourself as a religious person, the more you're going to look like a hypocrite if you're engaging in actions that at one point contradict your religious foundation." The authenticity of one's spirituality is often acted out rather than verbalized. Dillon said, "I'd rather have people see my spirituality than to be telling them about it all the time."

Most older books within the Christian tradition claim an ecclesiastically informed definition of "spirituality," focusing on pneumatology, or the work of the Holy Spirit. Newer writings, beginning largely in the 1960s, claim a much broader definition of the depth and flexibility of "spirituality" as it is understood across religions, cultures, generations, and identities.[7] For example, Ewart Cousins defined spirituality

---

7. For a more extensive discussion of how spirituality is defined, see chapter 3, pages 77ff. and the footnotes there. See also Anderson, Hill, and Martinson, *Coming of Age*.

as referring to "an ultimate or an alleged immaterial reality."[8] Philip Sheldrake provided a more personalized definition: ". . . the deepest values and meanings by which people live."[9] The term has been used recently to suggest a whole series of possible connections: to a fuller and healthier sense of one's inner life and self, or to other individuals and communities with mutual interests; to nature or the larger cosmos; or to various understandings of a nonhuman guiding force that is interested in the wellbeing of individuals and of humanity as a whole. Above all, it was clear from the students that very few restricted the concept of spirituality solely to the established religions of the world. As Aaron observed, "Spirituality is one's set of beliefs and actions and how those line up with religion, or not, and a relationship with God or whatever is out there. My own spirituality includes some questions about whether God is real or not." Some of the other interviewees were similarly eager to distance themselves from organized religion. Miguel's words articulated the difference: "Spirituality gives you more creative ability than does religion. I would never call myself religious."

Of the thirty-six interviewees, just over half defined spirituality as an expression of the value of caring for others rather than focusing on the self. Some of these respondents had clearly been deeply influenced by the Christian ethos of their schools, particularly by what they had learned of the Franciscan and Benedictine traditions. Aaron defined the component elements of a healthy other-focused spirituality as "Catholic social teachings, stewardship, hospitality, and tending to God's physical creation." Dillon was adamant about the other-focused connection: "Spirituality is nothing if it's not connected to social justice." Morris and several others argued that it is impossible for one's spirituality to be healthy without subscribing to social justice issues such as Fair Trade and more humane labor practices in the Third World. To Abe, it was the success of the Franciscan tradition in bringing about social change that made their spirituality so much more appealing than their religious practices. As Jerome argued, "Our spirituality should be better grounded in our relationship to others. I've learned that from my independent reading and my group discussions, not from any theistic notion of the

8. Ewart Cousins, "Preface," in Antoine Faivre and Jacob Needleman, eds., *Modern Esoteric Spirituality* (New York: Crossroad, 1992) x.

9. Philip Sheldrake, *A Brief History of Spirituality* (Hoboken, NJ: Wiley-Blackwell, 2007) 1–2.

Big Man in the Sky. Spirituality must be based on relationships, not doctrinal obedience."

For many who expressed their commitment to social justice, the fact that humans are created by a loving God or higher power obliges us to live out that love in the form of taking care of Planet Earth and going out of our way to help others, whether a friend, a family member, or those who are socially and economically disadvantaged. Many of the students reported their own active participation in acts of social justice, volunteering to serve in various capacities in such activities in their home towns, in the geographical area of their colleges, and overseas on summer holidays or year abroad programs.

Some of those interviewed acknowledged the connection between their outward-facing spirituality and their professional goals in life. For example, Blain said, "Social justice is very important to me, and is why I want to travel abroad and eventually to work with children." Steve struck a more domestic tone by observing, "I want a career that every single day I can go home and say, 'I thought about the needs of others today.' This is the direction my spirituality is moving in." Most of our research participants had been or were still involved in some sort of social service, including working in a homeless shelter, collecting food for the needy, working with younger less-advantaged children, and putting pressure for change on the present political order.

The other respondents—just under half—articulated a spirituality that was more self-concerned than other-concerned, though the definitions articulated seemed to imply that the proper forms of self-concern would eventuate in a world that was better for others to live in. Thus, their egocentrism was tempered by a concern for the way that their fellow students, their families, and the victims of social injustices would benefit from a spirituality that started "at home." Even here, their language often reflected a vocabulary that might have been influenced by the Christian heritage of their schools—journey, transcendence, etc. These respondents took a highly individual approach to defining spirituality. For example, Brice said, "Spirituality is about learning who I am and am not. The spirituality I practice is a blend of eastern and western traditions." Blain observed, "Spirituality for me is kind of knowing who you are and knowing partially where you want to go and where you've been and tying them all together into a philosophy of life." Beau summarized, "I define spirituality as 'what you do with whatever flows inside of you.'"

Comparing spirituality with masculinity, Colin observed, "Spirituality is sort of the same introspective examination that you would have in the masculinity realm, but it's broader. So instead of saying what does it mean to be a man, you're saying what does it mean to be human."

Oh course, for most of those interviewed, there was also an aspect of spirituality that they claimed as having particular appeal because of their experiences in their families of origin and their emergent values as young adults. For example, Keith remarked, "Spirituality is very personal and individual, and expresses the deep underlying connection of human beings to each other." Most of the research subjects were unwilling to pin down where the commitment to searching for a healthy spirituality might lead them. Dillon observed, "Spirituality should concern everyone because it's the pursuit of what really matters, but when you begin to pursue spirituality, you're not always sure what you'll find," and Jeff offered, "Your faith or sense of spirituality is a life-long journey, and people should not be too quick to pin everything down."

Even those who denied a commitment to theism found themselves attracted to acts of social justice. Nelson made just that point: "Even an atheist has a spirituality—if by that you mean a sense of social justice." Tom observed, "I think that an atheist can have a spirituality. I think my best example of this is when we talk about good works. Those who have good works have more faith than they realize." Later in the interview, Tom described himself as an atheist who is committed to the Summary of the Law. Not all of the participants linked social justice to the Christian tradition: Tom, who had already commented on his commitment to social activism, went on to remark, "I would define spirituality as really the recognition and acknowledgement of the Other, whether you call it God, whether you call it Buddha, whether you call it a Hindu name." Marc defined it differently: "It's a relationship—almost maybe a relationship with yourself, and maybe your relationship to anything that you find transcendent to yourself." Max observed that "[A]ll religions are just extensions of one greater spirituality underlying humanity. Spirituality is a way to unify people, not divide them."

A few of those interviewed struggled with the use and meaning of the term spirituality. Adam remarked ironically, "If you say you're religious, people think you're closed-minded, and have to follow the Bible to a T, like not wearing mixed cloth. But if you say you're spiritual, some people might think you're a hippie." Yet the interviewees were grateful for the opportunity to articulate where they were so far in their spiritual development as young men, and the opportunities for honest exploration provided by the men's spirituality groups. Miguel expressed his gratitude by saying, "I'm more open with my spirituality here than I might be any-place else." Above all, their spiritual explorations were grounded in their everyday life at college. Nelson affirmed this when he said, "Spirituality is not about what you believe, but what you're experiencing."

Some of the young men found their time at college to be their first opportunity in life to explore spirituality as an aspect of their daily lives, away from family and, in some cases, their home church. Aaron admitted, "My spirituality began to evolve when I found Catholic social teachings here." Yet others used the exploration of their emerging spiritual life to distinguish it sharply from religion. For example, Adam said, "Spirituality means there's some part of your life that's out of your hands. It's not the same as being religious. Spirituality helps you understand what you can change and what you can't, and how to be comfortable with yourself. Religion doesn't do that." Vince offered a parallel observation: "What spirituality means to me is just not from a religious standpoint, but from, like, living your life the right way, and looking back, and not having to answer or be ashamed of anything that you did because you did something wrong, or were on the wayward path." Ted put it simply: "Questioning myself and others deepens my spirituality."

Spirituality Does Not Equate to Religion

Adam's sharp distinction between spirituality and religion was echoed by three-quarters of those interviewed. Students argued that people did not need to be religious to be spiritual, and in fact, being religious was often detrimental to one's spiritual exploration. As Alan argued, "Spirituality needs to break its ties with religion to be taken seriously."

Some interviewees attempted to hold religion and spirituality to-gether, but the relationship between the two was tense. Adam noted the difference by saying, "I'm spiritual because I'm religious, but religious seems so much different from spiritual. People who are spiritual seem so much more laid back than people who are religious." To some of these students, the institutional church was rigid, uncreative, demanding, and oblivious to their needs and concerns. Adam went on to say, "I can't opt for religion only because I need to leave open the possibility that there are many things in the universe that we don't understand." Beau felt it would be much better to hold the two apart because the church is destructive: "Every human being is spiritual, but some get it mixed up with religion. Spirituality is about doing something constructive with our desires."

In spite of living and studying in religiously sponsored institutions, the students seemed to inhabit a world that had reservations about the church as it was being presented to them. As Colin put it, "Some of my closest friends are deeply spiritual but have little or no desire to be involved in religion." Jeremy echoed the same thought: "Religion is like a strict following. Spirituality includes having religious beliefs, but I know lots of people who don't go to church but are some of the most faith-driven people I know. Apparently, a lot of people don't need church." An involvement in discussions about spirituality offered a chance to help the students locate themselves within the transcendent. Jace said, "I stopped going to church as a young teen, and instead of rejecting that particular spirituality, rejected all spirituality. I'm now rethinking that." He went on to explain, "Religious faith discourages inquiry and thereby compels people to do some really bad things. Religion seems to have only one answer to everything, but spirituality offers several different answers to work out."

Some students were aware of what appeared to be elements of hypocrisy in the church. Jace pointed to those who "seem to be acting religious for political reasons rather than spiritual reasons." Later, he added, "The church says love your neighbor, but it means only if your neighbor is someone the church approves of." Miguel observed, "A lot of churches, in my experience, just don't deal with the hard issues that we become interested in in college. They just open the Bible and say 'Think this way.'" Miguel explained the lessened appeal of the church as follows: "Religion, as it's often quoted, is something that you can just do on Sunday mornings. Spirituality doesn't have a place and a time or a location in which I express my spirituality, from 11:00 to noon every Sunday morning. So it broadens this personal notion of myself." These students seemed to find the church's self-presentation to be off-putting and unattractive.

Spirituality is Bigger than the Church

Jeremy thus pointed to a common impression of the church among these young college males, many of whom had been raised in the church, or at least until their teenage years. Alan had that experience.

I was confirmed—given confirmation—when I was seven, at the same time I was getting communion. As I got older, I guess a number of experiences made me certainly question my faith, but then also seeing the fact that I was confirmed at seven, pledging allegiance to something that I didn't have any real understanding. I still believed in Santa Claus and the Easter Bunny when I was seven. Religion, I think, becomes—specifically, religion becomes alienating to a lot of kids. If you're not this, then you can't be a part of that.

Jeremy had a somewhat similar experience with his childhood friends: "A lot of my friends went to Catholic schools and came away sick of the prayers every day, and they're sick of dealing with crosses everywhere, and it drove them away from their faith." Miguel confessed to becoming less religious after arriving at college: "When I started here, I was—I mean, I was more religious than I am now. I would say that I'm not religious much anymore. But I still—I would still say I'm a spiritual person." Brice seems to have summed up the argument of other students about the way the church was presenting itself: "Talk is cheap, and many religions say the same thing, even though they act like they're competing." What the students heard the churches saying was not always attracting them to participate. Keith articulated why he couldn't find his way into the church any longer: "Religion becomes very negative when it becomes all about maintaining its own structure and power. When the church got into the business of leading armies, you can only ask 'What the hell's up with that? Where's the spirituality in that?'"

Churchgoers as Hypocrites

About one-quarter of the students interviewed commented on what they saw as hypocrisy in the church or among their fellow students who identified as Christians. Darrell commented, "I am troubled by all the people at college who appear to be pious Christians, but don't like questions to be asked. God sometimes seems more forgiving than other people are." In particular, narrow dogmatism among members of the church bothered the interviewees, summed up in Jeremy's comment, "One thing that really drives people my age away from church is the rigid Christian piety that some others like to display in public." Yet, Morris remarked on the hypocrisy which is sometimes exhibited by people who opt out of the church, too: "Certain people are dogmatic about their particular religion and then don't support something like Fair Trade or better labor practices for people in the Third World. But the same hypocrisy upsets me in people who have a more general spirituality."

Alan noted that "[w]e, the young, don't like the dogmatic form of religion that's been handed down to us. The traditional language of the church sounds more like Santa Claus and the Easter Bunny. . . . I can respect religion as long as it is not institutionalized or forced on me. Mostly, it has been detrimental to my spirituality." Adam commented not only on the hypocrisy in the church, but as well on the disinterest of the professors in his college in connecting the Bible more closely with the everyday culture in which students lived. "Some of the clergy seem to preach certain things but don't practice them. We notice the hypocrisy. And the school asks us to take courses in Bible, but never asks us how much we have learned about the Bible from popular culture. It would be great to have a free-based course on spirituality and let us hash it out."

Steve agreed with the point about hypocrisy, saying "I think it's a good thing to go to church. I think it's a good thing to practice some sort of religion, regardless of what it is. I just think there's a lot of hypocrisy." Keith went one step further: "Sometimes it's difficult to distinguish the power of the church from the power of terrorist leaders. That covers up all genuine feelings of a nourishing spirituality." Jason commented on how far religion and spirituality seem to have moved from each other: "Religion as commonly practiced today, especially in this country, is a joke. Religion and spirituality seem to have divorced and are drifting further and further apart." The "divorce" between religion and spirituality, and the seeming inability of certain churches to meet the students where they are, was leading to a growing disinterest by students in the church. Darrell observed, "As I grow older, I find people of other nationalities and ethnic groups and religions more interesting, while the majority of my family has become more narrow in their Christianity."

Two research participants in particular commented on the decreasing authority that clergy they have encountered in local parishes have. Abe described his youthful experience this way: "In the church I went to before college, the priest sorta mumbled all the time, and was just quiet, and you couldn't hear him half the—it was—I didn't know, I mean, just really what religion is—an older guy stuttering into a microphone." Max said, "I appreciate the ideological power of the teachings of the Catholic

Church but I don't think that many people buy into the spiritual power and authority of priests anymore."

Jason offered perhaps the most extended critique of the institutional church:

> A lot more people are seeing religion as a disorganized manifestation, as almost a political organization making its decisions on issues of extreme importance based on financial incentives and based on demographics and conversions. At Christianity's beginning, Christ was preaching and he sounds like he was probably talking about some good things. But as soon as he died, people started using the things he said to influence others for their own financial gain. Whether or not Jesus actually was the son of God, he probably did a lot of good things that moved people, and like I said, that's the most pure that religion has been but it was quickly corrupted for human gain.

Research participants also seemed cognizant of "the battle for the Bible"—the conflict among premodern, modern, and postmodern interpretations of Scripture within the churches. As Drew observed, "Two people can be equally committed to the Bible but interpret it differently." Students were aware that interpreters read many portions of Scripture very differently from each other, and seemed disappointed that the church didn't help its members become more open to seeking the complex meanings of so many biblical passages. Miguel said, "I think that a lot of churches, at least in my experience, don't deal with the hard questions. They don't open the Bible and look at the inconsistencies and ask, 'Why?' They open the Bible and say, 'This is God's Word.'" But Steve also held the faithful (including himself) responsible for the vast ignorance of Scripture in the United States. "As many times as I've tried, [the Bible is] a long book. I've taken it on plane rides and gotten twenty-five pages through the Book of John and said, 'This is the most boring thing I've ever read in my life!' I just want to read a children's Bible or something. But I think there are a lot of people like that, who just [read the Bible] when they have to. Like, 'Dear God, I need something now,' when they didn't need anything before when everything was going good for them."

Valuing All Religions as being Equal

At least one-third of our participants commented that they assessed all religions as being equally valuable, thereby opting not to give priority to

Christianity, even though all but one came from a childhood background of exposure to Christianity. Max admitted, "I like the Judeo-Christian idea of religion and spirituality. At the same time, I believe that all other faiths are valid. I see—often times when I compare religions, I don't see any crossover that prevents them all from being true." Steve was even more forthcoming:

> I feel like other religions, like Muslims, Buddhists, stuff like that—they put a whole lot more into their religion than the typical American Christian does—in my eyes. I think it's a good thing to practice some sort of religion, regardless of what it is. They're all based on good beliefs for the most part, other than suicide bombers and stuff like that. I'm sort of in an exploration phase where I want to know more. Not to say that I'm questioning God or religion or anything like that; I'm not hardcore science or hardcore creationism. I, personally, believe in evolution and personally believe that God can exist at the same time.

Of the thirty-six interviewees, six found Buddhism to be as valid a belief system as Christianity, six others found Hinduism equally valid, and three affirmed the importance of both Judaism and Islam, though a larger number of our participants than that spoke of the power of the three monotheistic religions.

Steve's equating of creationism and evolution echoed the opinions of about half of our research participants, in the sense that they discussed finding God in many places outside organized religion. For the most part, this was within nature in a variety of ways. As Jace said, "Spirituality is about the natural world and the natural world is where we seek answers." Adam also expressed the importance of nature in his understanding of spirituality, saying: "The classical spiritual experiences don't appeal to me but the mysteries of nature affect me deeply." Colin agreed, remarking how many of his spiritual experiences came "from nature and taking time alone and just being outside, or being inside just spending some time in quiet reading or whatever." Max was more explicit: "I find my spirituality confirmed in the primal beauty of nature," as was Nelson: "I'm connecting spiritually when I sense God in some way, shape, or form. I often do that in nature." Others spoke about feeling spiritually inspired when they were in the company of others, or when they were expressing themselves through music. As Mark said, "I can pray, but I find meditation tough. I often explore my spirituality through singing or playing the piano . . . or perhaps just thinking back over a day when I've worked hard."

It might be that this locating of spirituality outside the church was a factor among those interviewees who preferred the term "higher power" over the term "God." The higher power could be found in many places. Adam found his higher power within mathematics, perhaps not unlike the early Greek philosophers who believed that the world was made of numbers. Jeff seemed to find the term higher power to be synonymous with God, saying "My higher power is God, but everyone has his or her own spirituality." He admitted that he felt in the minority by using the term. "A lot of my classmates in my religion courses would simply say God, but for me, I think it's just kind of a personal thing—saying higher power—because I know that I'm comfortable with what my higher power is." Morris seemed to argue that whatever name one calls God is not as important as valuing human interdependence. "I mean, if you were gonna take, particularly, the position that we are created by some other power, some superhuman—God, or whatever one person wants to call it—then that should come with the recognition that we are connected with each other." A few of the participants were unwilling to take a stand on personifying or anthropomorphizing God, while recognizing that "something" appeared to be in charge of the universe and our existence. Nate said, "Spirituality to me is being in touch with a higher power, being able to reflect on your life and have the meaning behind it, or why you think you're here, put on this earth. There might be a God, there might be something else." Jason was even less sure that the church or anyone else really understood God: "I think if there is any sort of a higher power, it is nothing like the one that you read about in the scriptures. I think that you can be certain of that."

Agnosticism, Uncertainty, and the Value of Questioning

A few of our participants identified as being agnostic or atheist, either while in college or prior to attending. These participants were very involved in defining the meaning of spirituality in a way that included a sense of "not-knowing" about the existence or omnipotence of God as defined in the monotheistic religions. Nelson argued, "Yes, I think an atheist can have a spirituality. I think a lot of times when you do something good for people, or another person, or a group of people, like volunteering, for example, that makes you feel spiritual because you're helping the common good." For these participants, spirituality was more about a connection to humanism than to theism. Bart articulated that point: "I'm not a religious person at this point in my life. I was born and raised Catholic. And then around winter break of my freshman year, I really decided that I—where I was at in life I couldn't—I couldn't be calling myself Catholic anymore. So I kind of always say I'm an agnostic humanist." Jeremy, however, admired the drive and focus of his atheist friends:

> Spirituality is having something to believe in to guide you along the way, whether it be God, or whether it be a guardian angel. I know some friends who have that, and these are atheist kind of nonreligious people, but they have a drive. They have something. Not that I look down on people who don't have religion or don't have a faith, but I say, "What's guiding you through your life? Is something driving you? Is something—is it just all you?" They're, like, "Yeah, it's just me." It hasn't really hit my mind, and then I'm thinking maybe there's a reason why they're like this now.

Max defended agnosticism as a spirituality, although he would not put atheism in the same category. "In my opinion, an agnostic could have a spirituality but an atheist could not. An atheist, by the mere definition, subscribes to the idea that there is no greater power out there, and so it's hard for me to fathom an atheist being able to say that they're spiritual because, to me, spirituality may not imply a god but it does imply a faith of some kind, and to me, atheism doesn't include faith in anything except maybe the material." Sometimes, their respect for atheism was shaped by having an atheist friend who lived a life they admired. Vince said, "My best friend, who is very much atheist and doesn't believe in anything besides the human being, and anything like that, but morally, he's one of the best people I've met. He has a spiritual and moral character that is unique." Jerome found it difficult at college to defend the atheism he had chosen: "My spirituality? I wish it could help me communicate better some days. You know, it's, sometimes my spirituality or the way I feel in my spirituality, it's very difficult maybe to explain. And I just wish there was an easy communicable way to get it out, and get it out in a way that doesn't scare off people. Because normally as soon as you mention, I don't . . . I don't know . . . I don't rely on a theistic God, people are like, 'Oh, you are an atheist, sinning cynic.' And my spirituality is no longer communicable."

One participant, Keith, blamed the church for the rise of atheism among the young: "I get a sense that a lot of atheism is a lot of reaction against, especially in our time, against perceived injustices and Christianity and sort of tending to completely throw off *all* spiritual matters and so in that way I think atheism can be really damaging to you because I know, personally, this sort of spirituality is giving me a deeper connection to people." Jason appeared to agree in several ways: "I think a lot more people are seeing religion as a disorganized manifestation, as almost a political organization making its decisions on issues of extreme importance based on financial incentives and based on demographics and possible conversions—strengthening their own church and membership numbers and I think that that kind of gives rise to a lot of atheists, a lot of people who are annoyed about that." Yet, his participation in a spirituality group had moved him to a new spiritual stance. Tom, who had previously identified as atheist, described his own journey back to a more theistic position in this way: "Like I said, obviously, I was an atheist for most of my life. Even after I think my faith started, what I call my first turning point, I still showed demonstrations of atheism, as my roommate continues to remind me of [by citing] my first demonstration with him."[10] On the other hand, Dillon was critical of anyone he knew whose spirituality was devoid of all sense of the divine: "I have friends who are atheists who I think are very self-deceiving. That is their religion you know? Their sole belief in, I mean, just basically the human spirit, they end up being humanists with a capital H; that's how I understand them. So spirituality is trying to seek proof and then not buying it. Or any truth, just pursuit. I like the word 'pursue' because you may not even know what exactly you're pursuing but you're pursuing it and it affects how you live."

Yet even agnostics and atheists felt welcome in the college spirituality groups and saw benefit from their participation. With pleasure, Tom told his story of being invited to join such a group. "I was an atheist at the time we had had that [recruiting] dinner. I said to myself, like, 'This isn't going to work out.' I'm, like, looking at this, like, 'This is—No, but you kinda have an interesting point of view on everything,' and I think that I was also in a Christian gaming community; I still am, but

10. Tom described his faith as "agnostic," but he believed that God is love: "To be spiritual, whether it be, again, the Christian God or the Hindu God or the Muslim God, whichever faith or way you want to look at it, to me it's the showing of that love."

I recently joined [the men's spirituality group] now at the same time, because 'You could bring such an interesting point of view.'"

THE SUPPORTIVE NATURE OF THE GROUP EXPERIENCE

These young men were articulate about their journey through identifying their masculinity and spirituality, and expressed their gratitude to the programs that were provided for them by the chaplaincies at their schools. Abe told his story in detail.

> It started off getting a recommendation in our mailbox from somebody, and we didn't really know who, but it just invited us to a dinner, explaining what the idea of this group was, why we did stuff like this. So, it just kinda got us interested in this, and I was definitely interested right off the bat. So, we formed a little group of some people at that dinner who were interested, [along with one of the professors and a staff member from the chaplaincy], and we meet biweekly to discuss different problems and issues or how we feel about certain things. We start every meeting off with the best and worst of the past two weeks. So, we each go around and talk about it, and if it's something interesting or it's something that pertains to the topic we're going to discuss, we delve a little more deeply into it, but after we do that, we just talk about an issue that we had set from the time before. For example, right now we're working on, "How has God shown himself to you or not?" and we look at, compare, different people's ideas and how that explains their spirituality, or not, if that's the case. It's an interesting perspective to look at each different person, to see how they compare to you, how they don't compare to you, and it's also gone with the idea of men in general that a lot of times they don't share things—that in this forum, there's an opportunity to do that that they wouldn't normally have or would be too embarrassed to do. So, it's nice. I really look forward to the meetings every other week. It's a time to relax. I'm sure every other participant would say the same thing. It's comforting. It's a good thing to do, and especially if you have a big workload that week, it takes a lot of stress off. I mean, it's fun to participate in, and getting into [the process] was not a problem at all.
>
> The men's spirituality group, especially, shows me that there are a lot of ideas within the Franciscan community and within the realm of God and faith and spirituality that coincide with everything that I had been looking at before. I think I'm the better person for it and I'm glad to have this opportunity with a

group like that. I'll still acknowledge that I can't be sure if there is or is not a God. To be honest, I don't think there's any way to prove that there is or is not, so I mean, until somebody can, I suppose I'll have to remain somewhat in the middle, but I know that whether or not I believe that there is a God, I believe that my spirituality has grown, and my trust in the fact that there might be a God has increased dramatically in the time I've been here, especially through hearing some of the stories in the spirituality group.

Coming here and listening to stories through this group, I've realized that maybe there's some things that, regardless of whether there's a God or not, are out of my control. So, that's changed the way I look at issues. I control what I do, but not—and I realize I can't control—what others can do.

Abe's experiences with the men's spirituality group were echoed in so many ways by the other research participants from all seven colleges. Nate told his story this way.

Normally you don't meet guys that have your similar interests or live like you. So you kind of filter across that way, where coming into a spirituality group, you don't know these guys. Maybe you know one or two, but you really don't know these guys, so I think confidentiality is huge because you don't really know them and you can't trust them right off the bat, and if you want the group to work, you definitely have to have that confidentiality. I can tell you my whole life story and you can get to know me, but you're not going to tell this to anybody else. So I think that's a key component, especially when you don't know who they are at all.

I think the men's group is probably number one for me, just being able to hear everyone's story, and then also them talking about their relationships with their dad or their mom; it definitely—you definitely can relate to that. They've definitely had the same experiences that you have. Maybe you and your dad weren't that close growing up, but now you're getting better. Or you don't talk about your feelings with your dad. Hearing that from other people definitely is like, "Oh, okay, other people have that same experience and it's okay." You can work on that from the masculinity side. And my number one thing [is that] I love hearing about other people's spirituality and what they consider what their faith is, because I think a different perspective is always new and kind of changes and molds your own spirituality. That's one thing I wish we could add in our group is a little more diversity in where people come from; if we had some people that were international students or something who had a totally different perspective on spirituality, I think that would be really cool to get that. Just because I think the more that you know about different spiritualities and different people's perspectives, I think the better you understand your own. So definitely this group has fostered my masculinity and spirituality.

I knew I was joining a spirituality group kind of thing, but the aspect that I really didn't see coming was how close the camaraderie with the guys became, how close you can become with them because you've heard all these aspects of their life and you've heard what they believe in, too, and I feel like—when we went on that retreat and we hung out, and it was, like, awesome; everything clicked together. You trusted these guys, and now you're just hanging out with them, and I didn't see that camaraderie coming that we could just hang out and just have fun, you know what I mean? So, I think that was the aspect that I didn't see getting out of this group: just a whole new group of friends. Another thing about the group, I think I've expressed it before, but for me, the reason I joined it is because it was way more open. It wasn't religiously affiliated; it was open to any ideas and any thoughts. I kind of like the aspect of that and just it started off the first year about sharing your life and how maybe spirituality has come into play or hasn't, and when you get to hear other people's experiences, you definitely look past when you first walked into that room, that first judgment that you get with people. Once you hear all the tough things that they've done or the great things that they've done in life, you definitely get a new perspective on that kind of guy.

Young men from the various groups each brought their own perspectives and recollections, their critiques and appreciations. Some explained specific elements that made the men's spirituality groups work well for all those involved. For example, Adam suggested that "if you want to get guys to participate, it seems like you have to kind of get rid of as many limiting factors as possible." He commented upon the differences that eventually emerged within the apparent initial similarity of guys who found the group model attractive.

I mean, there's this certain type of guy that kind of gets into groups like this. So it's been kind of interesting to see even the kind of the subtle differences between that particular subset of guys that are willing to participate in this group. I know that I'm one of the many who's not overly religious, so I think that was kind of a draw just because of the whole retreat thing and how they kind of got their people. To start the group, they got their people from retreat, but now we have recruiting nights. But it's just been interesting the way that we approached recruiting and our message of trying to define masculinity and obviously that's not confined to one particular type of guy.

Alan, from yet another college, described a different recruiting process for membership within the group.

One of the professors ran up to eight of us and said, "We're gonna try this. Let's see if it works." It's worked for eight so far, so it was . . . We defined spirituality in general as anything that has the ability to move an individual or a group of people, something that may be sacred more than human, may transcend human qualities, but transcend the earthly realm in a sense, but not necessarily tied to religion. Our group is not in any way tied to Christianity, Judaism, Islam—nothing. It's that which mystifies an individual, is able to move them, keeps them interested, and something they're compelled to continually learn about, in a general sense. Specifically, it's manifested in a number of ways across our group. In general, I think the time we spend together has become very spiritual each week. In order for all of us to get to know each other and spend time together, to see how each of us are moving each other, we've done weekend retreats in upstate New York, which we've all found very spiritual, and sacred for us—a very sacred place. It's the barn.

Last week, we talked about our fathers, describing our relationship with our father, who our father was, and the week before that, we talked about what we look for out of relationships with significant others, whether it be a man or a woman. We talked about the spiritual—what we find spiritual. We've gone political, which didn't last very long, then philosophical. "What does it mean to be a man?" usually gets brought up each semester as the group changes and as we grow. We'll see varied themes on the lives of the young men, sometimes, what we'd like to see improve at the college, but basically centered on our own lives.

On each of the campuses where we did research, it was obvious that the men's spirituality groups appealed to only some of the male students. This did not escape the notice of our interviewees, including Colin:

I think there's a disparity, at least on this campus, and I would imagine also as well that there is a group of men who think about masculinity and have their ideas about what it is to be a real man. And they're usually pretty involved and they put a lot of energy into issues of masculinity and spirituality and things that really matter. And then there's another group that sort of just doesn't care or is too busy living the college life to really think about it. I guess that's how I see it, but I sort of surround myself with men who are in the same group that I am.

Beau seemed not to understand why the groups didn't have a wider appeal when he observed, "It doesn't necessarily take a special kind of person to be in one." Yet, this splitting of men on campus into at least two groups was echoed by several of the men interviewed, emphasizing that the groups often became the genesis of their own social involvements outside the program.

Brice commented on the intimate and supportive dynamics in his group:

> For me, it's been a very good experience in that it's a group of guys I can trust. I know I can go to talk about whatever's bothering me, explore issues I hadn't really thought of before, and help other students do the same thing. They're my friends; I want them to feel comfortable enough to bring up these tough subjects, whether they be family issues, health issues, faith, mental, whatever. I want them to feel comfortable just like I feel comfortable, and I think it's good that we're all able to be at that point now where we can, and I think it was really set that first year because we just sat down and said "Tell us your story" in those group meetings, and that was really hard for some students who had never been part of that kind of experience, and now we're all at that point where we're comfortable. It's been a great experience for me, sharing something new, something needed.

Jarad felt that the spirituality element was in fact strengthened by the group's character, as though a healthy spirituality couldn't be accomplished to its fullest by an individual alone. "Spirituality to me is to understand yourself in order to connect with other people, to be spiritual as a group instead of an individual. But you need to know yourself first. So it's more—it's individual at first, but then to complete the spirituality, I feel like you need to have a group to connect with other people using your own spirituality."

The groups were characterized by discussion on a wide range of topics, which of course broadened their appeal to the students. Jerome observed that "[m]any students look for spirituality groups that are not closed-minded," while Jace expanded further on that subject:

> We try to come up with a discussion topic at the beginning and that is pretty much up to anyone. The group is not really led although an administrator handles the budget. It's not really led in any particular manner by one person and anyone could suggest a topic and so we discuss that until it's basically reached a point of exhaustion and then it could be anything from, like, our experiences with men on this campus to, you know, something that is bothering us politically or philosophically or something that is interesting to us spiritually. It really doesn't take any form. Yeah, it is just pretty casual and relaxed.

Keagan described the dynamics in his group by noting that it had become a place where he felt comfortable enough to talk about his inner thoughts and feelings because he had grown to know the others in the group so well.

> But you know you're comfortable talking to those guys because they might have something to say that would help you out. Like, oh you can take this class because you know you need that credit anyway, or this might be a good class for you to experience because you might find out that you like this subject and that subject. You know you'd probably experience that with your academic advisors and people of that sort too but . . . There's— each meeting that we have is kind of, like, I don't know, because each—pretty much each time that we get together, either one individual is sharing or we're all sharing something that we experienced, either over spring break or just at some point in our lives or you know we're getting back from Christmas break and we have stories to share and whatever. And so it's personal because it happened to us and it's sometimes private because it was a good thing and sometimes private because it was a bad thing, or something like that, so yeah, there's, like, there's vulnerability because you might not want somebody to say something about what you talked about just because it was hard to share. It was a difficult experience, like you broke up with your girlfriend, or if you lost your grandma or grandpa or something like that, or a parent, and you share that and the guys in group are respectful and they listen. You don't want them to share with anybody but you feel vulnerable and you know they won't because they've all shared something. So probably, there's, like, that mutual secrecy, you know, I'm gonna tell you something, so in respect . . . But

yeah, that's the best thing about the men's spirituality group and, yeah. It's awesome I think—I mean, everybody shares their kind of personal stories or opinions.

Garett emphasized that the groups might not appeal to everyone, anyway. "What's good about having a good group of guy friends is when they're intelligent and they're not just meatheads or that stereotypical, you know, so then you can have a discussion, like a spirituality discussion."

Miles described what he thought were the three most important outcomes of the group in which he participated:

> We needed some sort of outlet for men to go and talk about guy stuff. And there just wasn't a place for that. So the groups started—understand, it's kind of adapted throughout the year-and-a-half right now where we're at. It's kind of a three-part mission. First, we as a group are a space for members and non-members—anyone can come in and it's a safe, confidential space for guys to open up and talk about anything they're dealing with—men's issues. Second, we want to get guys on campus more involved in service and spirituality, anything they're passionate about but that they might think isn't manly, I guess. And third, just a greater society than we are, and awareness of the things that society—ways men abuse power and the negative masculinities, I guess. So we've done stuff against abuse and rape and that kind of thing. So yeah, that's kind of our three-part mission.

An important quality of the men's spirituality groups, emphasized by all our research participants, was safety. Ted put it this way:

> Just by having a safe zone, I'm more willing to, even outside of the spirituality group, to, I guess, place my views on what I believe in spiritually and I guess not worry so much about what—like an alternate view or someone thinks it's ludicrous, that type of thing. So, I guess, just me coming to terms with my spirituality is what's changed. I guess not the terms but just knowing that that's what I believe in and not letting anyone tell me otherwise. I think it does help when you do say it is confidential. But even outside of spirituality group, a lot of the people in my spirituality group I consider friends. And I feel that whenever I guess someone brings up an aspect of spirituality group that I mean wouldn't have to be like confidential, maybe just like I was . . . I get the feeling that they know what and what not to say about the situation, so not to [expose anyone].

Research participants talked about the connection between the groups and the wider academic and chaplaincy staff on their campus. Adam remarked, "I can say I've learned certain aspects of masculinity from teachers and other interactions I've had with male figures here at college." Drew went into more detail: "The religion and the spirituality pop up everywhere and it's sort of—every class that I've taken has somehow tied in with religion or spirituality. I find that most of the faculty here are also themselves religiously involved and spiritual. And outside of it, either within or outside of the classroom, depending upon the context of the class, they are willing to engage in conversations with students about practically anything. And so, yeah, I definitely see that as being very evident here at the university and in its mission and in the way that they go about directing classes and activities on campus. Definitely yes." Tom talked about how his group experience had built a bridge to the campus chaplaincy that helped him through a couple of tough times. "I've grown in spirituality group by being able to discuss those issues that are tough in regard to problems that are the common denominator among men, but not necessarily among all females. So I'm very glad of that. I also want to emphasize that I've loved my experiences in the group as a whole. I mean, even, like, when my father fell off a ladder, or more recently, when my father had a minor stroke."

There are a few rules that bind the men's spirituality groups. Confidentiality has to be discussed, and then thereafter assumed, in order to build trust. The composition of a group projects de facto a certain definition of masculinity; as Adam pointed out, "not every man on a campus will want to participate in a group like this, for the childishness of high school has to be left behind." Among other characteristics of a good group member is the young man's choice to cooperate with the purpose of the group—(as Blain observed, "Men don't thrive in college without direction from the outside")—i.e., his willingness to let down his "front," to open up in trust with others whom he will see outside the group in various settings on campus. As Jason put it, "In the group, there's not really any of those masculine fronts you were talking about. We're just talking about trying to be men." Members of the group don't have to be best friends, but they do have to participate in the creation of a unique kind of bond that allows for trust and confidentiality. In the group, young men discuss "unmanly" things, such as feeling uncomfortably pressured to "do masculinity" in a certain way, not to question stereotypes and expectations, to be honest even when that honesty produces feelings of failure and shame, to live with and relieve the suffering of others. Yet as Bart observed, "Crises are easier when you have a group to support you that understands what you're talking about. Men understand men in a way that women never can." For Colin, the support and encouragement of a men's spirituality group was invaluable as he went through the ups and downs of young adult male life: "Masculinity is something that's deeper than religion, even deeper at the core of men. It's something that I feel has been stifled a lot in our culture. Being a real man with authentic masculinity is about defying that, breaking the norm, standing up for truth and justice and what is right and being opened to that introspection and not forcing your views on other people."

LINKING MASCULINITY AND SPIRITUALITY

The young men who participated in the interviews were articulate, open, courageous, and self-revealing. Interestingly, of all the topics they were encouraged to address in the live interviews, the greatest diversity appeared in the area of the relationship between masculinity and spirituality. About 20 percent said there was no relationship between the two, about 30 percent said that a deepened and more respectful sense of masculinity increased one's spiritual health, and about 50 percent said that a deepened and more creative spirituality led to increased health in one's gender identity as masculine.

There is no Significant Relationship between Masculinity and Spirituality

Vince felt caught between the worlds of two different masculinities—the "tough guys" and the men in his group. Of the tough guys, he said:

> I don't know if it's like being vulnerable, or being, like, judged. I just physically can't tell people, and that's the same with my friend. He says the same thing. He's like, "There's some things that a lot of my friends . . . ," and some guys won't even talk about their inner world, because it's the whole masculinity thing. I don't know. They're like tough guys. Like I said, I've been on the wrestling team in high school, and a lot of them—and they're my best friends—and a lot of those guys have been, like, really, like, tough in nature. Like manly man, I guess, and they just—to have a spiritual conversation with them would be—it'd be futile. It just

wouldn't occur. [They'd say] "Quit being a pansy," or something like that, so that kinda thing. So, I think it's just when you're, like, in that type of environment, and I feel the same kinda disconnect. I think it's because I'm not as close to those guys. So, maybe that's why.

Drew, Nelson, and Steve, each from a different college in our study, couldn't see a connection between masculinity and spirituality, even after participating in the men's spirituality groups. Steve confessed, "I don't know that I could make a direct correlation between spirituality and masculinity. I'm sure that they're tied in some way, but I wouldn't say that I feel masculine when I'm doing something spiritual, or that I feel spiritual when I'm doing something masculine." Nelson didn't even connect God with masculinity, which seemed to make the connection between spirituality and masculinity that much more difficult for him. "I usually, I mean, I wouldn't normally connect masculinity and spirituality. I mean, I wouldn't consider being spiritual to be something that I can identify with also being masculine. What's interesting is that, at least in my religion, God is—I mean, God doesn't really have a sex, but traditionally, the way that he's depicted in paintings and things like that is male." Drew rejected the connection for yet a different reason: because he saw spirituality as an integral part of his character but saw masculinity as a label put on him from the outside by others:

> Because I am masculine, or consider myself masculine and because I consider myself spiritual, they are, then, of course, intertwined. Does my spirituality necessarily signify or point out my masculinity in a way? No, probably not. Again, going by social construct, do I feel that it is entirely okay to be masculine and spiritual? Yeah. Do I think that the two should coincide? Yes. But as far as their being—as far as being structurally related—probably not so much. I consider spirituality as being something that I am. Masculinity or masculine is something that I consider that other people sort of label me as. And we use that label to distinguish many things. I consider masculinity to be more of a label or a category in which you fit, whereas spirituality is something that you are that goes across. It's not necessarily a label, it's you.

A Healthy Masculinity Promotes a Healthy Spirituality

The majority of our research participants—about 70 percent—found a connection between masculinity and spirituality, but differed among themselves whether an increasingly healthy masculinity leads to an increasingly healthy spirituality, or whether it works the other way around. In the former category, Miles argued that because people relate first to each other based on gender role, therefore gender role was more important in the building of human bonds. "It's hard to connect with people. And I think that's one of the reasons we do approach it from the masculinity avenue instead of spirituality."

Nate reasoned that spirituality proceeded out of masculinity, as a way of softening it and broadening it.

> In our culture, it's definitely the tough guy attitude, and for sure you know I play football. You see on the football team all the time that guys can't share feelings; you've got to be big, strong, and tough, be the basis of the family or whatever, so that's definitely how our culture portrays it. Definitely, like, "You shouldn't be showing your emotional side." It's a girly thing to show that. In terms of my masculinity, I feel like this group, in the men's spirituality group, I've tried to become more open and share my feelings and just a sense of touch like how in the group meetings we . . . I think that's also a thing that the [football] guys just have a handshake—it's never a hug, it's never a kiss—it's just a handshake. So I think our culture has kind of portrayed that, too. So I think in my own masculinity, I'm slowly changing, but I feel like I'm becoming more open with my feelings with other people and myself, and also being able to be open to everyone else, I guess.

A Healthy Spirituality Promotes a Healthy Masculinity

About 50 percent of our research participants, however, concurred that a healthy spirituality promotes a healthy masculinity, and therefore reasoned that the transformation needing to be focused upon was the identification of, and growth in, spirituality. Jarad argued that spiritual growth precedes and drives growth in gender identity: "To be masculine is to have everything under control. I feel like to be masculine is to know what you need to do, how you need to do it, what and—to know that you need to know yourself, what your boundaries are, and how you think and how you feel. So if you're more spiritual, I feel that you can better accomplish those tasks." Jerome agreed with him: "I think my spirituality would influence my masculinity more so than my masculinity would influence my spirituality. I value—I value my identity as male even though I might exhibit more feminine qualities on many more occasions in my lifetime than manly qualities. But I think most of who I am is determined by my spirituality."

Morris argued that a healthy spirituality was the basis upon which the actualization of expected gender roles was constructed.

> Spirituality is very important to masculinity. I mean, if you're just gonna take the position that you are a masculine man, and then there's X, Y, Z that you have to do—I don't think that you're really going to achieve a lot of that without spirituality. How are you going to be the provider for your family, which is—if we agree if it's a tenet of masculinity—if you don't have some spirituality of why you have to do that? What is your calling to be a good provider? For me, it would be my spirituality. It would be my . . . I have a responsibility to other people, particularly my family, and that's because I believe that we were all created in some image and likeness of supernatural beings, and that we should subscribe to some reality. So, I think that reflects on this masculine model of how you want to be as a man.

Nate identified how spirituality had taught him to be a better man: "I guess one of the forms of masculinity is being open to yourself and being open to others, and with your spirituality, that kind of fosters that. When I'm talking to God and sharing what I think and not holding anything back, I think that helps you stay true to yourself and helps you express those emotions. You're leaving it all right up front when you're talking to God. It helps you improve your masculinity almost, and makes you almost more of a man that you can be open with others and open with yourself."

Tom described the intimate relationships that had developed within his spirituality group, and these fed in to his sense of masculine charity toward others.

> They've come to me with some of their issues, very much spiritual issues, but also just life issues, seeking my advice. To me, that's where my spirituality and masculinity have been shown greatly. Seeing these kids, whether it be my younger brother or that idea, there's no point in everybody in this world making the same mistakes every time. If we can help each other out, we

would be able to drop down. I'm not saying we're going to fix everything, but we might be able to drop down some of those mistakes. I mean, to me, where I mix that kind of idea is in that of using the spirituality, using that loving idea, to build the masculinity, to build that responsibility, brothers. To show others a) how to help themselves, but b) the idea—I remember, recently there actually was a guy who I asked for a book. I wanted to know if anybody had an extra copy of the book *The Case for Christ*.[11] He mentioned to me, he goes, "Yeah, I've got an extra copy. Give me your address and I'll mail it to you." He goes, "Here's how you can repay me. I showed you kindness, I want you to show it to somebody else. When you get the chance, when you are blessed, I want you to bless someone else. When you get that chance, show it to someone else." To me, that's spirituality and masculinity. It's that idea of spreading that. To me, that would be my best kind of definition for how I would integrate the two.

Research participants agreed that being in touch with one's emotions was equally important to the growth of a healthy masculinity and a healthy spirituality. Alan summed up his thinking this way: "Masculinity is about being able to show emotions. Spirituality? There's a huge tie to our emotions. Aspects of spirituality include describing our relationships with our fathers, describing the influence of significant others, asking what it means to be a man; how the college could support our spiritual journey, our masculinity . . . These two things have converged on this one front."

Colin described how a combination of masculinity and spirituality had taught him how to treat others with the respect they are due.

> I guess I think of masculinity in terms of an attitude about the way you approach your life and the way you approach other people in your life. It has a lot to do with just the way that you see yourself interacting with others and the respect that you treat others with . . . and not just in an outward sense, but that you really take it to heart, and so, as a real man, you respect not only women and respect their equality and their benefits, their humanity, but you will also do the same for other men, and that you respect life and you have this attitude of trying to help others and being active in helping others. And that can come down to, like, a spiritual level, if you're a spiritual man, but it doesn't have to be

---

11. Lee Strobel, *The Case for Christ: A Journalist's Personal Investigation of the Evidence for Jesus* (Grand Rapids, MI: Zondervan, 1998).

because masculinity is something that's, I think, even deeper at
the core of men.

Operating out of a framework of the social construction of both
gender identity and spirituality, Adam spoke personally about his own
journey.

> I think both of those make up my personality, so yes I would say
> there is a connection between masculinity and spirituality. You
> can think about masculinity as maybe a certain belief set that
> defines a male and within that belief set would be some type of
> spiritual beliefs, so, I think for me, yeah, there would be a con-
> nection between the two, just because they are so intertwined
> that it's hard to—I mean, they just make up who I am as a person,
> so that if you were to separate them, then, you know, it would be
> almost creating a disharmony within myself.

Aaron summed up many of the thoughts expressed by the research
participants: "My spirituality and masculinity coincide when I understand that I am to be responsible to God, including by owning up to my
feelings and my understanding of the world. Maturity means building a
link between your masculinity and spirituality, so that you're cool with
both."

Yet, it was not unusual to find disagreements about masculinity
and spirituality even among members of the same spirituality group. The
groups were intended to provide a venue for exploration and discussion, but not to indoctrinate the young men into a particular theological
position, even though all of the seven colleges where the research was
conducted are church affiliated. Keagan raised an interesting example
of some ways in which both masculinity and spirituality can become
confused by a focus on traditional Christology.

> If I were to picture God as depicted as a male figure in the Bible,
> so logically kind of speaking, I would think of Him as being a
> him. So there's a masculine part about God because Jesus is God's
> son and Jesus was a man. To me, like I said, I see—I probably
> see God in other people. And so if I were to tie masculinity and
> spirituality together, it would be the fact that I know that when
> God sent His only son, it was a man. There's that . . . there's that
> masculine characteristic that permeates everyone, you know,
> that permeates through everybody. I mean, obviously, that sense
> of spirituality and masculinity that permeates everybody because
> if you believe in God, and not everybody does, if you believe in

God, then there is certainly a component of every person that is masculine and that is so—spiritual. So, yeah, it's difficult for me to tie together, to be real honest with you.

Keagan's logic was reflected by only two others among the thirty-six young men who were interviewed, yet such remarks suggest that the men's spirituality groups still may have some work to do with young men who come from those traditional Christian backgrounds that make gender equality and respect even more difficult to understand.

CONCLUSION

The intention of this chapter was to provide a broad, but well-illustrated, overview of what has been happening in the men's spirituality groups at seven of the fourteen colleges that were part of this larger study. While thirty-six young men were generous enough to allow us to tape interviews with them, there have been about 300 college-age participants in men's spirituality groups over two and a half years. Those young men embody the desire to find a relationship between their masculinity and their spirituality, and have found the men's spirituality groups to be a safe venue, not only to define what it means to be spiritual and what it means to be a man, and how those two categories fit together, but also have found that they are surrounded by other seekers who wish to walk a similar journey with them.

As these young men have formed their own groups on a particular campus, some of them have been aware that similar groups are being formed on an increasing number of college campuses across the country. They are, therefore, not alone in seeking new ways to engage transcendence and to act out their gender identity. In the next chapter, we will suggest some directions in which we think these changes are going in the future, and what challenges they are offering the church as it has been known traditionally.

5

Conclusion and Future Directions

THE THIRTY-SIX YOUNG MEN in our study had only one thing in common: they were all participants in men's spirituality groups that had been organized on small, religiously affiliated campuses in the United States. Aside from that, they exhibited a wide diversity of opinion within the recorded interviews on their experiences in defining their own masculinity and spirituality.

The effect of elite college campuses on the spirituality of young adult students has received significant attention recently. Two studies in particular support our own findings in the area of spirituality—that young men in private colleges and universities are more likely to move away from the "truth claims" of the institutional church and move toward a challenging exploration of their own very personal spiritual life and values.

In *Cultivating the Spirit: How College Can Enhance Students' Inner Lives*,[1] researchers Astin, Astin, and Lindholm surveyed more than 112,000 freshman in 236 public and private colleges and universities in 2004, and then followed up three years later with 14,527 of them from 136 schools, as they were completing their junior year. Their research affirmed the important role that spirituality can play in the lives of students as they learn and develop in the critical years of early adulthood, between the ages of 18 and 22. The authors defined spiritual development very broadly: "how students make meaning of their education and

---

1. Alexander W. Astin, Helen S. Astin, and Jennifer A. Lindholm. *Cultivating the Spirit: How College Can Enhance Students' Inner Lives*. San Francisco: Jossey-Bass, 2011. This study is discussed in this book in chapter 3.

their lives, how they develop a sense of purpose, the value and belief dilemmas they experience, as well as the role of religion, the sacred, and the mystical in their lives."[2] An alert reader will notice how little mention this description includes of organized religion, for indeed, as their study and ours showed, the more elitist the educational institution, the more likely young adults are to raise questions about the traditions of the church. As another piece of recent research pointed out, "Just as spirituality 'grows' in breadth of meaning, so does the term *religion* shrink, becoming increasingly narrow and restricted to traditional religious beliefs and organizations."[3]

Gall, Malette, and Guirguis-Younger summarized "spirituality" out of their own research, but their definition agrees strongly with our findings as well.

> In a content analysis of research definitions, Chiu, Emblen, Van Hofwegen, Sawatzky, and Meyerhoof (2004) identified our components of spirituality: (a) existential reality or meaning and way of being in life, (b) transcendence, (c) connection and wholeness, and (d) the presence of a unifying force or energy. Others have noted similar elements of spirituality with some additions, including a clearer identification of the element of a higher power or God. These definitions of spirituality move it beyond the traditional concepts of God and more toward the existential in life. Spilka's (1993) earlier observation that spirituality can be conceptualized in three main ways: (a) as linked to God and theology, (b) as it relates to nature, and (c) as linked to the humanistic concept of self-actualization.[4]

Their study does not, however, parallel ours, in that the research participants in the study by Gall, Malette, and Guirguis-Younger were not limited to college-age males in the United States, but rather, included 234 participants of both genders of a variety of ages and diverse nationalities.

In addition to the study by Astin, Astin, and Lindholm, the other recently published study whose findings parallel our own is that of Jonathan Hill, published as "Faith and Understanding: Specifying the

2. From a synopsis of the book at http://spirituality.ucla.edu/book/.

3. Terry Lynn Gall, Judith Malette, and Manal Guirguis-Younger, "Spirituality and Religiousness: A Diversity of Definitions," *Journal of Spirituality and Mental Health* 13.3 (2011) 158–81 [159].

4. Ibid.

Impact of Higher Education on Religious Belief" and based on his doctoral thesis.[5] Hill constructed his doctoral research on the National Study of Youth and Religion (NSYR), funded by the Lilly Endowment, in conjunction with the Integrated Postsecondary Education Data System (IPEDS). The NSYR and the IPEDS produced data from 3282 eligible respondents in a nationally representative sample. Research was conducted in three waves between 2002 and 2008. The first wave, in 2002–2003, covered students aged 13 to 17 years; the third wave, in 2007–2008, covered students aged 18 to 23.

Hill summarizes a number of research reports published in the last ten years, arguing that

> [t]here is evidence that the college experience may liberalize the theological beliefs of some religious students while simultaneously enhancing students' "inner" spiritual life. There is also increasing evidence that the influence of college is conditional on the subpopulation being studied as well as institutional context. For example, [I showed in my doctoral thesis] that religious affiliation and salience of faith increases among African Americans who attend and graduate from college, but that affiliation and salience of faith declines among college-going Catholics.[6]

As well, he observes another dynamic that may also have been at work in our research. "It may be, as recent surveys have suggested,[7] that a growing distrust of institutions has become a part of our common culture, and students come to campus already embracing an element of epistemological skepticism and cultural pluralism."[8] Hill concludes his article with the observation that

> [A]lthough college does not appear to substantially alter the religious beliefs of most emerging adults, findings do reveal a modest increase in skepticism toward super-empirical religious beliefs among college students and graduates compared to those

---

5. Jonathan Hill, "Faith and Understanding: Specifying the Impact of Higher Education on Religious Belief," *Journal for the Scientific Study of Religion* 50.3 (2011), 533–51. His doctoral thesis was entitled *Religious pathways during the transition to adulthood: A life course approach* (University of Notre Dame, 2008).

6. Hill, "Faith and Understanding," 533.

7. Pew Research Center, *Distrust, Discontent, Anger and Partisan Rancor: The People and their Government*. Washington, DC: Pew Research Center. Online: http://people-press.org/report/606/trust-in-government.

8. Hill, "Faith and Understanding," 547.

who have never attended any form of postsecondary education
. . . This change is most plausibly related to exposure to secular ideas, faculty, and possibly to identity work associated with
the elite social status of associating with these institutions . . .
[G]raduating from college modestly increases preferences for institutionalized religion while simultaneously reducing adherence
to exclusivist religious belief.[9]

Within the term "identity work," Hill would surely include the type
of "men's spirituality groups" that were researched in our study, including
the young men's opportunities in the groups to explore new definitions
of masculinity, and to seek ways in which their spiritual explorations
could support and enrich their search for new ways to act out their gender identity, both for their own health and for the great good of humanity. Our qualitative data supports the conclusions reached through the
quantitative and mixed-methods studies of Astin, Astin, and Lindholm;
Gall, Malette, and Guirguis-Younger; and Hill—and offers a significant
challenge to college and university offices of student life, classroom professors, campus chaplains, and indeed, to the parents of college-age men
throughout the United States.

LOOKING TO THE FUTURE

One way to respond to this challenge is to work creatively to develop
men's groups on campuses that will enable male students to have safe
places to explore their spirituality as a means to "know thyself." Saint
John's University was the first institution of higher education to explore
how this might be done, and their years of successful development and
maintenance of men's spirituality groups has provided a model from
which others have learned. Although we did not expect, nor did we find,
that other colleges or universities would be able to duplicate Saint John's
model without significant modifications to fit their own contexts, other
institutions did effectively adapt the Saint John's model to allow college
men in different institutional settings to explore their own spiritualities.

Because the spirituality groups on these various campuses had a
significant impact upon their participants, as our research has demon-
strated, we encourage additional campuses to explore the possibility of
establishing such groups. As interested persons consider this possibility,
it will be helpful for them to engage questions such as the following:

9. Hill, "Faith and Understanding," 533, 548.

- Is there a foundation within the institution that will undergird a men's spirituality program? If the institution has a mission statement, how can this statement be evaluated to determine whether and how the mission of the institution might provide a framework of values that could inform the development of the program?

- Have the persons working in institutions that are related to spiritual traditions explored how the values within those traditions might be interpreted to provide a framework that is open to any or no religious traditions? This would allow students to explore their own spirituality without their being expected to adopt a particular normative form of spirituality.

- If the program is developed within a secular institution or an institution of higher education that does not have a mission statement that could be used to provide a foundation for a program of spirituality groups, is there some other group that can take the initiative to develop the program? For example, is there a campus ministry program that might take the initiative to develop a men's spirituality program?

- Have those seeking to develop a men's spirituality program identified or created a mentoring community? Will it begin with faculty and staff of the college or university? Will the group facilitators themselves be willing to examine their own spiritual autobiographies in order to enable them to deconstruct the male gender role for themselves, so that they will be effective in assisting the men in the groups they facilitate to do this in their own lives?

There are additional questions that should be asked to determine some of the practical issues involved in the development and sustaining of a spirituality group program:

- Will the program begin small and then expand?

- How will the program be administered? What process will be used to select participants? How will group facilitators be trained and supported? What adaptations will be made to respond to the changing needs of those involved in the program?

- Will the facilitators continue to nurture their own spiritual development, and if so, how will this happen? Will they have periodic meetings with each other, retreats, or other forums to discuss common issues?

Additional considerations that are important for the internal functioning of the groups include:

- When a group is formed, it is important to make certain that it is regarded by all of its participants as a community in which it is safe to explore some of their deepest personal issues in an atmosphere that is supportive and nonjudgmental. At the outset the facilitators should explain the importance of confidentiality, commitment, and communication. If the group members function well, they will come to regard each other as part of a covenanted community and their time of meeting together as sacred time.

- Those in the group should be encouraged to regard their coming together, not as a forum to discuss abstract ideas, but as a community of men exploring their inner lives and examining their most important relationships. It may at times be possible to use a lecture or a book discussion as a way to draw college men to consider the possibility of becoming involved in such a group. Once a group is formed, the facilitators should encourage the participants to use "I" statements as they share their experiences and respond to others' statements.

As we look to the future, we believe that spirituality group programs can provide institutions with an opportunity to be on the "cutting edge" in contributing to the holistic development of men in the college learning environment. Such groups can be a way of responding to students' felt needs for opportunities to attend to the spiritual dimensions of their lives as they become part of structured groups that can help them challenge the restrictions imposed by traditional masculinity, freeing them to express themselves as persons.

A well-developed spirituality program can also provide other significant benefits to institutions of higher education. As colleges and universities encounter increasing cultural, ethnic, and religious diversity among students, a program of spirituality groups can be an effective means of community building, fostering a safe environment to explore and appreciate differences. Such a program can create opportunities for students to interact with faculty and staff to develop relationships that enable them to feel more at home in the institutions, since most students leave behind the networks of support they had in high school when they enter college.

Finally, we believe that the development of men's spirituality programs, appropriately adapted to draw upon the resources of the institutions and to meet the needs of the men on the campuses in which they are implemented, can provide a way for men to connect more fully to themselves, to other men, and to significant others in their lives. Such programs can be one means, among others, to contribute to the holistic development of men to enable them to be more integrated within themselves and in their relationships with others.

Appendix

Research Methodology

THIS STUDY SOUGHT TO explore the interrelatedness of masculinity and spirituality as interpreted through the lived experience of the traditional-age college male. It investigated the understanding of masculinity and spirituality among eighteen- to twenty-two-year-old college males and the ways in which men's groups and the group dynamic might help college men better integrate these two dimensions into their lives.

Traditional-age college males are exposed to diversity in thought and experiences, in and out of the classroom, that may lead to a critical reevaluation of beliefs and behaviors. This self-discovery takes place in the context of how a young male understands himself to be masculine and may influence how these two elements, masculinity and spirituality, are experienced and pursued. Masculinity and spirituality can both be strong influences in the individuation process of the young male, and greater understanding of the compartmentalization or integration of masculinity and spirituality may provide insight for personal growth and development in the college-age male.

The qualitative research for this study was conducted at seven private colleges and universities in the United States. The approach to qualitative research followed in this study uses the grounded theory methodology developed by a number of theorists, including Glaser and Strauss,[1]

---

1. Barney G. Glaser and Anselm L. Strauss. *The Discovery of Grounded Theory; Strategies for Qualitative Research* (Chicago: Aldine, 1967).

Strauss and Corbin,[2] Silverman,[3] and Patton.[4] In this chapter, we will give a rationale for choosing qualitative methods and the grounded theory approach, describe the design of the study, and outline ways in which rigor and verification were maintained.

RATIONALE FOR QUALITATIVE RESEARCH

According to Miles and Huberman, "Qualitative data, with their emphasis on people's 'lived experience,' are fundamentally well suited for locating the meanings people place on the events, processes, and structures of their lives . . . and for connecting these meanings to the social world around them."[5] Qualitative research is multimethod in focus, involving an interpretive, naturalistic approach to its subject matter. This means that qualitative researchers conduct studies in their natural settings, attempting to make sense of or interpret phenomena in terms of the meanings that people bring to them. Qualitative research involves the studied use and collection of a variety of empirical materials that describe routine and problematic moments and meaning in individuals' lives.

Qualitative research can be defined as "any kind of research that produces findings not arrived at by means of statistical procedures or other means of quantification."[6] Such research produces findings determined from real-world settings where the "phenomenon of interest unfolds naturally."[7] Qualitative research is undertaken in the environment in which the persons being studied live and work, and seeks to understand phenomena in that context-specific or "real world setting and the

2. Anselm L. Strauss and Juliet M. Corbin. *Basics of Qualitative Research: Grounded Theory Procedures and Techniques* (Newbury Park, CA: Sage, 1990).

Anselm L. Strauss and Juliet M. Corbin. *Basics of Qualitative Research: Techniques and Procedures for Developing Grounded Theory*, 2nd ed. (Thousand Oaks, CA: Sage, 1998).

3. David Silverman, *Doing Qualitative Research: A Practical Handbook.* (Thousand Oaks, CA: Sage, 2000).

4. Michael Q. Patton, *Qualitative Research and Evaluation Methods*, 3rd ed. (Thousand Oaks, CA: Sage, 2002).

5. Matthew B. Miles and A. M. Huberman. *Qualitative Data Analysis: An Expanded Sourcebook*, 2nd ed. (Thousand Oaks, CA: Sage, 1994) 10.

6. Strauss and Corbin, *Basics of Qualitative Research: Techniques and Procedures*, 17.

7. Patton, *Qualitative Research and Evaluation Methods*, 39.

researcher does not attempt to manipulate the phenomena of interest."[8] Such research seeks to understand phenomena within persons' lives, lived experiences, behaviors, emotions, and feelings.[9]

Undertaking qualitative research requires considerable time and resources because it is necessary for the researcher to engage personally with the population being studied. Such engagement in the field can extend over prolonged periods of time, usually months and sometimes even years. Data can be collected through group observation and in-depth interviews, but might also include documents, films or video-tapes, or literature, as well as other types of data,[10] all of which produce a considerable volume of materials to be analyzed. Referring to this type of in-depth data collection, Patton claimed that "the researcher is the instrument" by which data is collected.[11]

Masculinity and spirituality, the foci of this study, are areas of young men's lives that are oftentimes personal and deep. Qualitative research methods offer several advantages when studying the complexities of young men's lives,[12] and grounded theory is an effective research tool for mining the meaning of multifaceted issues. In the gathering and analysis of data about the personal, lived experiences of these young men, this approach seeks to understand the meaning or nature of experiences and what people are doing and thinking.[13]

Grounded Theory and Data Analysis

Developed by Glaser and Strauss in 1967, grounded theory allows theory to emerge from the data. When there are a number of individual experiences to be compared and contrasted, each individual's experience is written up, and the researcher begins to search for patterns across these individual experiences.[14] Grounded theory, then, can be described as a theory that

8. Ibid.

9. Strauss and Corbin, *Basics of Qualitative Research: Techniques and Procedures.*

10. Ibid.

11. Patton, *Qualitative Research and Evaluation Methods*, 14.

12. Sally Hutchinson, William Marsiglio, and Mark Cohan, "Interviewing Young Men about Sex and Procreation: Methodological Issues," *Qualitative Health Research* 12.1 (2002) 42–60.

13. Strauss and Corbin, *Basics of Qualitative Research: Techniques and Procedures.*

14. Patton, *Qualitative Research and Evaluation Methods.*

is discovered, developed, and provisionally verified through systematic data collection and analysis of data pertaining to that phenomenon. Therefore, data collection, analysis, and theory stand in reciprocal relationship with each other. One does not begin with a theory, and then prove it. Rather, one begins with an area of study and what is relevant to that area is allowed to emerge.[15]

This type of comparative analysis can be used to develop two sorts of theory—substantive, and formal. Their distinction and location within the broader concept of theory is important.[16] Substantive theory is developed for an empirical "area of sociological inquiry, such as patient care, race relations, or professional education."[17] In contrast, formal theory is developed for a conceptual "area of sociological inquiry, such as stigma, deviant behavior, formal organization, socialization, reward systems, or social mobility."[18] Formal and substantive theories fall between the "minor working hypotheses of everyday life and the all-inclusive grand theories."[19]

SUBSTANTIVE AND FORMAL THEORY

While distinguishable on levels of generality, substantive and formal theories differ only in degree, and in any one study share similar points with one another.[20] Therefore, it is important to point out that this study focused on the substantive area of the interrelatedness of masculinity and spirituality, with an emphasis on how these might be influenced through men's groups. The generation of this theory was achieved by a comparative analysis between and among data within this substantive area, as suggested by Glaser and Strauss.[21] This process of comparative analysis was carried out through open, axial, and selective coding, a detailed, line-by-line analysis with the purpose of developing internal

---

15. Strauss and Corbin, *Basics of Qualitative Research: Grounded Theory*, 23.
16. Glaser and Strauss, *Discovery of Grounded Theory*.
17. Ibid., 32.
18. Ibid.
19. Ibid., 33.
20. Ibid.
21. Ibid.

categories and relating them among categories, which grounds theory in data.[22]

CODING

Data gathered during the interview phase of this study were examined and reexamined in a process that Strauss and Corbin call microscopic examination, or coding. This microscopic examination is not a structured, static, or rigid process. Rather, "it is a free-flowing and creative one in which analysts move quickly back and forth between types of coding, using analytic techniques and procedures freely and in response to the analytic task before analysis."[23] While the coding process is free-flowing, there is nonetheless a structural microscopic examination approach that guides the coding process of open, axial, and selective coding.

Microscopic examination is detailed, line-by-line analysis, or coding, of data gathered throughout the study with the purpose of developing internal categories and relating them among all emerging categories. Coding, then, is the process of careful and close examination of the data transcripts in the study. As the researcher becomes more familiar with the data, categories began to emerge. Words, phrases, sentences, or even paragraphs are sorted within these categories during the interrelated yet distinct levels of open, axial, and selective coding.[24]

Open Coding. The desired outcome of open coding is to "break open" the data to uncover, name, and develop concepts, and expose the thoughts, ideas, and meanings contained within the text. This first analytic step of systematically pulling the data apart creates the framework for the analysis and communication that follows.[25]

Axial Coding. Axial coding begins the process of reassembling data that was sorted during open coding and linking categories with other categories, or around an "axis." During axial coding, categories are related to their subcategories as a more precise explanation of the phenomenon begins to emerge. This process includes laying out the properties of a category, identifying the variety of interactions, and looking for "clues"

22. Strauss and Corbin, *Basics of Qualitative Research: Grounded Theory.*
23. Ibid., 58.
24. Ibid.
25. Ibid.

as to how categories might relate to each other. During the process of axial coding, the researcher begins to formulate a more precise explanation of the theory emerging from the data and continues the process begun during open coding.[26]

Selective Coding. Selective coding refines and integrates the theory that begins to emerge and "begins to build up a dense texture of relationships around the 'axis' of the categories being focused upon."[27] As analysis continues, major categories are interpreted to form the larger theoretical scheme, and these take the form of theory.[28] This integration and refinement of the categories takes place through the process of interaction between the analyst and the data. "Brought into that interaction is the analytic gestalt, which includes not only who the analyst is but also the evolution of thinking that occurs over time through immersion in the data and the cumulative body of findings."[29]

DATA COLLECTION

Semistructured Interviewing. The semistructured interview insures that the basic line of questioning is consistent when a number of participants are being interviewed. The semistructured interview provides a guide to the topics and subject areas, while allowing the researcher freedom "to explore, probe, and ask questions that will illuminate the particular subject being explored."[30] The interview guide also helps insure effective use of time during the interview because it ensure that the questions have been well thought out and follow a systematic exploration of the issues with a number of different participants.[31]

By the very nature of qualitative research, all researchers will have some degree of emotional involvement in the subject of study, and researchers should be cautious about the degree of such involvement. Conversely, complete detachment from the subject of research is neither achievable nor desirable, and the semistructured interview

26. Ibid.

27. Strauss, 1987, as cited in Strauss & Corbin, *Basics of Qualitative Research: Techniques and Procedures*, 124.

28. Strauss and Corbin, *Basics of Qualitative Research: Techniques and Procedures*.

29. Ibid., 144.

30. Patton, *Qualitative Research and Evaluation Methods*, 343.

31. Ibid.

helps researchers to be clear about their level of involvement and detachment.[32] The semistructured interview, then, is a useful tool to help strike a balance between the level of involvement and detachment of the researcher so as to minimize researcher bias.

Formulation of the Interview Guide. Because the interview guide significantly shapes the interview process and the subjects covered, it is essential that this guide be carefully developed.[33] The interview guide for this study was developed in several stages. We first met to discuss the study and what we would like to learn from the men we would interview. We developed a preliminary guide and shared it with colleagues and students, after which we discussed the insights of those we had consulted and made changes in the interview guide. After all thoughts and suggestions had been processed, a revised interview guide was developed. This resulted in an interview guide that shaped the interview process, took into account the balance between involvement and detachment of the researcher, and helped clarify researcher bias, as recommended by Creswell.[34]

Protection of Human Subjects. This study was conducted in accordance with the protection of human subjects and approved by the Institutional Review Boards of Saint John's University, Collegeville, Minnesota, and Siena College, Loudonville, New York. Participation in the study was voluntary, and participants were informed that they could withdraw from the study at any time. Prior to their participation in the study, participants received detailed information outlining the purpose of the study, their rights as research participants, and a list of possible questions that might be asked during the interview.

Before the interview, participants were asked to review a consent form and encouraged to ask any questions they might have about the study or the interview process. The consent form contained contact information about resources available for counseling if the participants had such needs. A signed copy of the consent form and a "Your Rights

32. Catherine Perry, Miranda Thurston, and Ken Green, "Involvement and Detachment in Researching Sexuality: Reflections on the Process of Semistructured Interviews," *Qualitative Health Research* 14.1 (2004) 135–48.

33. Patton, *Qualitative Research and Evaluation Methods.*

34. J. W. Creswell, *Qualitative Inquiry and Research Design: Choosing among Five Designs* (Thousand Oaks, CA: Sage, 1998).

as a Research Participant" sheet were provided before the interview commenced.

Confidentiality was maintained throughout the study. Consent forms, audio recordings, and transcripts were stored separately in locked files. Participant names did not appear on transcripts, and audio files and alphabetical numeric labels were used for identification purposes. Real names were not used in any report or analysis of the data.

Participant Selection. Participants were recruited for this study through contact persons at seven of the fourteen small liberal arts colleges that had participated in the Lilly grant, "Project on the Participation of Young Men in Theologically Grounded Vocational Exploration and Identifying and Implementing 'Best Practices.'" Students who responded were given additional detailed information about the study—including a consent form, "Your Rights as a Research Participant," and a list of the questions that would guide the semistructured interview.

Meeting times were set up in 90-minute blocks to allow sufficient time for unforeseen delays or lengthy interviews. At the time the interview was scheduled, participants were asked to review the interview questions and think carefully about them prior to the interview.

Interview Structure. In-depth, semistructured interviews used in this study allowed young men to open up and share complexities of their subjective lives and, in their own words, tell their story and make meaning of personal feelings and specific relationships.[35]

Interviews took place at times that was most convenient for the participants and were conducted on the school property. The rooms in which the interviews took place were "living room style" with comfortable chairs and couches, or classrooms or private offices. Interview rooms at all institutions were private but located in public buildings on campus.

Sufficient time was allowed between interviews so that when participants arrived and departed, they would not encounter other participants. When the participants arrived, they were cordially greeted and, after settling into the seats, participants were thanked for their participation and given the opportunity to review the consent form and the "Your Rights as a Research Participant" sheet, and were encouraged to ask any

---

35. Hutchinson et al., "Interviewing Young Men about Sex and Procreation."

questions they might have. When all questions and concerns were addressed, the participants were asked to sign the consent form and were given a copy of it.

After all paperwork and preliminaries had been completed, the audio recorder was turned on and the participant was reminded that the interview was being recorded. If the participant had additional questions in regard to any aspect of the study, he was invited to voice those concerns. The interview then commenced, and the questions that the participants had previously received were used as a guide for the semistructured interview. At the end of the interview, participants were again informed that the interview had been recorded, the recorder was then turned off, and the interview was complete.

DATA ANALYSIS

We listened to the interview recordings again and again. We were attentive not only to what was being said but how it was said with inflection, pauses, and emphasis in the voice, and constantly compared what we were hearing in one interview with similar things we were hearing in the other interviews, sorting out similarities or themes. We also read and reread the interview transcripts, paying particular attention to words, phrases, or statements and made comparisons of the same type of words and phrases in the other transcripts.

As we became more and more familiar with the data that had been collected in the semistructured interviews, we made notes and grouped words and phrases in the transcripts that were similar (or the same) and that might help us expose the ideas and meaning contained in the text. As we looked at these words in their larger context, we sought to understand what participants were trying to express. This was the open coding phase of the analysis.

Through the axial coding phase, we investigated how words, phrases, or passages might be similar or different within and among interviews. Were there categories into which we could place these concepts and emerging themes? As we sorted and compared the structures within the context of the interview, where the words and phrases of emerging themes occurred we attempted to expose the thoughts of participants by uncovering and naming the ideas and meaning contained in the data.

This process of data analysis or constant comparison through the coding process was fluid and organic. That is, one phase of coding did not neatly end when another began but, instead, one flowed out of the other. Sometimes we moved back and forth in the coding process as we uncovered and verified themes emerging from the data.

Computer Assisted Qualitative Data Analysis Software (CAQDAS)

The process of "shaking" words or pieces of meaning out of the data and constantly comparing the bits and pieces throughout all the data so as to discern the emerging meanings can become a tedious process. The disassembly, examination, and reassembling of data in verifiable themes can be a complicated and sometimes messy task. We were greatly aided in the coding and analysis process by the use of a computer software package. NVivo 7, developed and marketed by QSR International Pty. Ltd., Doncaster, Australia, was used to aid in the coding and analysis phase of this study.

STANDARDS OF QUALITY AND VERIFICATION

Standards of quality in qualitative research are "complex and emerging."[36] Howe and Eisenhardt (as cited in Creswell) suggested that only broad, abstract standards of quality and verification are possible for qualitative research. It is not surprising, then, that researchers do not agree on the importance of procedures for establishing and defining verification of qualitative research.[37] However, if any study is to be taken seriously, quality and verification must be clearly addressed.

Although standards for verification in qualitative research procedures are complex and diverse, consistency and clarity are necessary when addressing this important aspect of a study. To that end, we chose to use the systematic approach for maintaining standards of qualitative verification as outlined by Creswell. Creswell offers a working definition of verification "as a *process* that occurs throughout the data collection, analysis, and report writing of a study and standards as *criteria* imposed by the researcher and others after a study is completed."[38]

Every study has a unique set of variables and circumstances that may influence the reliability of data collected from participants and every researcher faces the serious challenge of ensuring that the data he or

36. Creswell, *Qualitative Inquiry and Research Design*, 193.
37. Ibid.
38. Ibid., 194.

she collects is accurate. While there is no reason to believe that we would be any more or less objective in our research, it is important to explore how our unique role could influence the reliability of the data.

The fact that the researchers in this study had extensive access to and familiarity with men's groups was indeed a great benefit to our research. However, this advantage notwithstanding, we were concerned that we, as older men who were college professors and administrators, might influence the responses we received from participants. Would young men be open with us about their spirituality and personal experiences? Might they fear some sort of judgment/evaluation on our part and therefore tailor or filter their responses accordingly? Were we getting valid data?

We were concerned then about how we could evaluate the quality and content of our interviews. Were we receiving accurate information from our participants? Could we verify that we were? To answer these questions, we utilized a proven and systematic approach that other respected researchers have used to assess the quality of the data gathered through semistructured interviews.

Hutchinson, Marsiglio, and Cohan have conducted research on young men's understanding of sexuality and procreation, and their study shared many similarities to ours. They had studied young men and had used a semistructured interview for data collection. The age and sex of their participants were similar to the participants in our study, and they too were asking questions of a personal nature. Hutchinson, Marsiglio, and Cohan, asked the same question about their data that we asked about ours—that is, how do researchers know they have gathered verifiable and truthful information? They answered this question by systematically evaluating their own research techniques and establishing six criteria for evaluating the quality of semistructured interviews: emotional accessibility; view of interviewer as counselor; collaborative behaviors; declarations of comfort; detailed, dense, personal information; and narrative revisions.[39]

EMOTIONAL ACCESSIBILITY. Hutchinson, Marsiglio, and Cohan concluded that rapport seemed evident when the young men in their study exhibited emotion/positive affect during the interview; joking, laughing, or providing information with a very serious demeanor in almost con-

---

39. Hutchinson et al., "Interviewing Young Men about Sex and Procreation."

fessional tones; hanging around after the interview; or spontaneously commenting positively about the interview or interviewer.

Participants in our study frequently stayed after the interview and asked about the study and its progress. Numerous men expressed interest in the project and a desire that fellow students could participate in what they felt was a positive experience.

VIEW OF INTERVIEWER AS COUNSELOR. When the participants view the interview process as helpful or even therapeutic or indicate positive feelings toward the interview process and a belief in the interviewer's good will and potential to help, researchers know they are collecting valuable data.

Participants in our study frequently expressed appreciation for the opportunity to take part in the interview. We ended each interview with the invitation to add anything that might be on their mind that they wanted to say but had not been asked, or to express anything that might have come to mind. At times, this was some of the richest information from the interview. It was also a time in which participants frequently expressed their thankfulness for the opportunity to take part in the interview.

COLLABORATIVE BEHAVIORS. Participants in Hutchinson, Marsiglio, & Cohan's study appeared to take the role of a collaborator. A feeling of mutuality or that the participant had joined the team seemed to prevail. In our study, many participants also expressed a desire for their male friends to be involved, or a desire that more men could participate in the men's group experience.

DECLARATIONS OF COMFORT. The participant gives spontaneous feedback to the interviewer. Declarations of comfort indicate that the researcher is on the right track and that the participant is at ease.

Participants appeared relaxed and comfortable in taking time to answer questions. Sometimes they would think for long periods, 15 to 20 seconds or more, as they attempted to understand and express feelings. As we listened and relistened to interview recordings, these pauses were apparent throughout the interviews. Participants also struggled to share not only their personal experiences of masculinity, spirituality, and the group dynamic but also their understanding and interpretation of these experiences, and they expressed comfort in doing so.

DETAILED, DENSE, PERSONAL INFORMATION. When participants provide rich, detailed information about topics that are sensitive, socially unacceptable, or that do not reflect positively on themselves, the researcher can feel confident that he or she has been able to obtain quality data.

Participants in this study gave deep and personal information about their inner emotional and spiritual life. Some men volunteered aspects of their sexuality and relationship with a significant other, even though these questions were not part of the study and were not asked.

NARRATIVE REVISIONS: Participants revise their statements during the interview process, reflecting a desire to be accurate. Our participants frequently revised a response or revisited a previous section of the interview in which they felt they had given the wrong impression.

Applying the methodology and six indices outlined by Hutchinson, Marsiglio, and Cohan, we felt assured that the data received from the interviews was as credible as that of any other careful researcher and that our role as professors and administrators did not negatively influence our results and may even have been an asset.

Suggestions for Further Reading

FATHERS AND SONS

Biddulph, Steve. *Raising Boys: Why Boys Are Different—and How to Help Them Become Happy and Well-Balanced Men.* Berkeley, CA: Celestial Arts, 1998.

Gurian, Michael. *A Fine Young Man: What Parents, Mentors, and Educators Can Do to Shape Adolescent Boys into Exceptional Men.* New York: Jeremy P. Tarcher/Putnam, 1998.

Pollack, William S. *Real Boys: Rescuing Our Sons from the Myths of Boyhood.* New York: Henry Holt, 1999.

Pollack, William S., and Todd Shuster. *Real Boys' Voices.* New York: Random House, 2000.

GENDER

Barash, David P., and Judith Eve Lipton. *Gender Gap: The Biology of Male-Female Differences.* New Brunswick, NJ: Transaction, 2002.

Barnett, Rosalind C., and Caryl Rivers. *Same Difference: How Gender Myths Are Hurting Our Relationships, Our Children, and Our Jobs.* New York: Basic Books, 2004.

Butler, Judith. *Gender Trouble: Feminism and the Subversion of Identity.* New York: Routledge, 1999.

———. *Undoing Gender.* Boca Raton, FL: Routledge, 2004.

Connell, R. W. *Gender.* Short Introductions. Malden, MA: Polity, 2002.

———. *Gender and Power: Society, the Person, and Sexual Politics.* Stanford, CA: Stanford University Press, 1987.

MASCULINITY

Brod, Harry, ed. *The Making of Masculinities: The New Men's Studies.* New York: Routledge, 1987.

Clatterbaugh, Kenneth C. *Contemporary Perspectives on Masculinity: Men, Women, and Politics in Modern Society.* 2nd ed. Boulder, CO: Westview, 1997.

Connell, R. W. *Masculinities.* 2nd ed. Berkeley: University of California Press, 2005.

————. *The Men and the Boys.* Berkeley: University of California Press, 2000.

Kimmel, Michael S. *Manhood in America: A Cultural History.* New York: Free Press, 1996.

————. "Masculinities." In *Men and Masculinities: A Social, Cultural, and Historical Encyclopedia*, edited by Michael S. Kimmel and Amy Aronson, 503–7. Santa Barbara, CA: ABC-CLIO, 2004.

Kimmel, Michael S., and Amy Aronson. *Men and Masculinities: A Social, Cultural, and Historical Encyclopedia.* Santa Barbara, CA: ABC-CLIO, 2004.

Kimmel, Michael S., and Michael A. Messner. *Men's Lives.* 8th ed. Boston: Pearson, 2010.

Kimmel, Michael S., Jeff Hearn, and R. W. Connell. *Handbook of Studies on Men & Masculinities.* Thousand Oaks, CA: Sage, 2005.

Stepnick, Andrea. "Making Godly Men: The Social Construction of Masculinities in Promise Keepers." PhD diss., Florida State University, 1999.

SPIRITUALITY

Anderson, David W., Paul Hill, and Roland D. Martinson. *Coming of Age: Exploring the Identity and Spirituality of Younger Men.* Minneapolis: Augsburg Fortress, 2006.

Astin, Alexander W., Helen S. Astin, and Jennifer A. Lindholm. *Cultivating the Spirit: How College Can Enhance Students' Inner Lives.* San Francisco: Jossey-Bass, 2011.

Boyd, Stephen B. *The Men We Long to Be: Beyond Domination to a New Christian Understanding of Manhood.* San Francisco: HarperSanFrancisco, 1995.

Boyd, Stephen B., W. Merle Longwood, and Mark W. Muesse. *Redeeming Men: Religion and Masculinities.* Louisville, KY: Westminster John Knox, 1996.

Chickering, Arthur W., Jon C. Dalton, and Liesa Stamm. *Encouraging Authenticity and Spirituality in Higher Education.* San Francisco: Jossey-Bass, 2006.

Culbertson, Philip. *New Adam: The Future of Male Spirituality*. Minneapolis: Fortress, 1992.

————, ed. *The Spirituality of Men: Sixteen Christians Write About Their Faith*. Minneapolis: Fortress, 2002.

Longwood, W. Merle, Mark W. Muesse, and William Schipper, O.S.B. "Men, Spirituality, and the Collegiate Experience." In *Developing Effective Programs and Services for College Men*, edited by Gar E. Kellom, 87–99. New Directions for Student Services, No. 107 (San Francisco: Jossey-Bass, 2004).

Nelson, James B. *The Intimate Connection: Male Sexuality, Masculine Spirituality*. Philadelphia: Westminster, 1988.